William R Orr

The Dominion Accountant

Or New Method of Teaching the Irish National Book-keeping

William R Orr

The Dominion Accountant
Or New Method of Teaching the Irish National Book-keeping

ISBN/EAN: 9783744739252

Printed in Europe, USA, Canada, Australia, Japan

Cover: Foto ©Andreas Hilbeck / pixelio.de

More available books at **www.hansebooks.com**

THE DOMINION ACCOUNTANT,

OR

NEW METHOD OF TEACHING THE

Irish National Book-keeping,

BY

WILLIAM R. ORR,

PRINCIPAL OF THE MERCANTILE ACADEMY,

AUTHOR OF
"THE MOST COMPLETE SYSTEM OF COMMERCIAL AND LADIES' WRITING,"

AND AUDITOR OF THE CORPORATION OF THE CITY OF TORONTO, ONT.

Authorized by the Council of Public Instruction for the use of Schools in the Province of Ontario.

PUBLISHED BY A. DREDGE & CO.,

53 Yonge Street, Toronto.

1873.

PREFACE.

AFTER twenty-six years' experience as a Practical Accountant and Teacher, I have ventured to introduce to the favorable consideration of the Canadian public "The Dominion Accountant," or "New method of teaching the Irish National Book-keeping."

A thorough examination of all the larger, and even smaller standard works on book-keeping, within my reach, led me to the conclusion, many years ago, that the Irish National was the best fitted for the school-room as a text-book; and my varied and extensive practice since, both as a book-keeper and a teacher of the science, has served to convince me that that conclusion was a just one.

In the plan, it is more progressive than any book on the subject with which I have met. It begins at the beginning, and proceeds by regular gradations until it reaches the highest order and most intricate description of accounts.

The first set teaches, in a few Cash transactions, simply how to Debit and Credit, that is, on which side to enter the Cash received, and on which that paid out, without any regard to ulterior results; in fact, how to keep a Cash Account. The second set has a Cash Account like the first, and in addition introduces Personal Accounts, by which means the pupil is instructed how to make the Contra entries in the corresponding accounts, viz., to Debit the Cash Account with the money received, and Credit the person's account from whom it was received, and *vice versa*. The transactions are so arranged that the three Personal Accounts in this set, with two or three entries on the Debit and Credit side of each, serve the purpose of as many hundreds or thousands of such accounts; because all the results that can possibly arise in the management of personal accounts, are produced. At the winding up of the set it is found that one of the persons is indebted to me, that I am indebted to another, and that, in the case of the third, the Debit and Credit sides are alike; neither of us, therefore, owes each other anything—all that could possibly be learned, respecting the results of personal accounts, from a book of a thousand folios. And both sets are so short that they can be thoroughly mastered, the first in one evening, and the second in two at most, thus laying the foundation of a practical knowledge of book-keeping in a few hours. In like manner the other sets proceed, each set becoming more and more difficult as the pupil progresses, until a complete knowledge is obtained of the most difficult entries connected with any commercial transaction.

Such, however, is not the mode adopted by authors generally. The pupil is put to work to write out, at first, a complete set of books, containing many pages of transactions, all of which he cannot possibly remember, and of whose nature and bearing he can know but little, if anything. Add to this the difficulties of opening and closing a set of books, and he has a task set him too difficult to surmount, and which even persons with some practical experience might fail to satisfactorily accomplish; but yet it is supposed not too great an undertaking for the raw student and the unpractised Dominie to perform. And with what results? Simply the production of a bad copy of the author before them—nothing more.

The nine sets, in the present small work, are not only short, but every entry is designed to produce certain results, and these results are as varied as the fluctuations of commercial life. In closing the second set, it will be found there is neither gain nor loss—the merchant ends as he began; but his property is somewhat differently situated, and this the pupil should be made clearly to understand. In the third and fourth sets there is a gain, and the fifth ends in a loss. The sixth and seventh* sets, which contain the most varied, practical and difficult entries to be met with in any work on the subject, both result in a gain. Intentional mistakes are made in the sixth set, such as Charging merchandise to the wrong person, and Crediting the wrong person for payments made, for the purpose of teaching the pupil how to rectify them. Great advantages accrue to the learner from the shortness of the sets, as well as from the comparatively large number of them. Their brevity enables the pupil to carry all the transactions in his memory from the first to the last; and their number not only gives great variety, as regards the nature and position of the merchant's property at the opening and closing of each set, but also much practice in opening and closing the books, a thorough knowledge of which is so indispensable, that, without it, all the other information that can be acquired on the subject is comparatively valueless.

The "Irish National Book-keeping," in its original form, is in sterling money and British weights. I have substituted for them the decimal currency and weights. It contains eight sets of books; I have rejected the last set, called the "Farming Set," because I consider all specialties in book-keeping a waste of the pupil's time, and likely to impress the mind with a wrong idea, viz., that a special business requires special principles of book-keeping, whereas, the truth is, the principles of book-keeping need only a special application to the peculiar business.† I have therefore retained only seven of the original sets in the present work; but I have added to these the *fifth* and *sixth* sets in a varied form, for the purpose, in the first place, of showing the advantages of "Single Entry," by changing the fifth set—Double Entry—into Single; and in doing this, I have introduced an Expense Account, and retained, in a modified form, the Profit and

---

* The eighth set in the present work.

† The books which proclaim too many methods of book-keeping, as well as those who profess to teach them, are alike untrustworthy. In every possible variety of book-keeping the principles are identical. When, in advertisements relative to this subject, we find teachers professing to embrace, in their course of instructions, all knowledge on all matters relating to every possible variety of commercial pursuits—Book-keep-*ing*, Bank-*ing*, Railroad-*ing*, Steamboat-*ing*, Telegraph-*ing*, and even Debat-*ing*, (without SPELL-ING and READ-ING), until the most astounding climax of INGS is reached that ever fell under the eye, or upon the ear of mortal man! Oh, save us from these everlast-*ing ings*.

PREFACE.   v

Loss Account,* as in the Double Entry method; and have produced results, in closing the set, equally as satisfactory by the Single, as by the Double Entry system, and with a great deal less work. In the second place, as all the sets in the original work are journalized entry by entry, and day by day (a good method for the learner), I have given the sixth set in the collected form, according to the most approved practice of the best Mercantile Houses both in the Old Country and in the New Dominion. By pursuing this plan in the class-room, I have enabled many young men in Toronto, in thirty or forty hours' instruction, who were totally ignorant of book-keeping at the commencement of these lessons, to take charge of, and keep the books of some of the largest and best managed Wholesale Houses in the Province—proof sufficient of the practical merits of the "Dominion Accountant."

I have not altered the text or interfered with the questions at the end of the sets; but I have appended notes where the text seemed to require it, and trust these will be found instructive and useful. I have also prefixed the questions and answers on the principles and practice of book-keeping, used in my lectures to my own students; these the pupil should learn thoroughly before commencing to write out the books, and they should be rehearsed as often afterwards as the teacher can make it convenient—say once a-week.

In the "Compendium of Merchants' Accounts" will be found Rules showing how to *Debit* and *Credit* every description of Entry that can possibly occur in any department of the Commercial circle.

I have not multiplied Books of Form, for the obvious reason that every mercantile house has its own peculiar forms; and to the man who understands the principles of the science, *forms* are of but little account. I have, however, given in an appendix a few forms of Notes, Bills, etc. Also some Arithmetical Rules, especially applicable to commercial pursuits—the one for Equating Payments, or averaging notes; those for converting Sterling Money into Halifax and Decimal Currency and *vice versa;* and those on Exchange, with the form and manner of working the interest on an Account Current; the Abbreviations, Signs and Explanations of Commercial Terms, etc., will, I doubt not, prove acceptable to the mercantile community.

Accountants, engaged in any business whatever, will find this treatise very valuable as a book of reference. It is so arranged that, at any point in their progress, they can find an exact counterpart, and, by turning to it, may at once verify their work.

Having thus endeavored to explain the contents and practical bearing of the "Dominion Accountant," I leave its fate to the decision of that public from whom I have already received so many tokens of favorable consideration and regard.

Toronto, 1st June, 1868.   WM. R. ORR.

---

* It is most remarkable that a Profit and Loss Account is not to be found in any published Single Entry Set of Book-keeping I have seen. See note, page 173, fifth set, Single Entry.

PUBLISHERS' PREFACE

FOR

SECOND EDITION.

The "Dominion Accountant" has stood the test of criticism better than any other work on Book-keeping that has either been published in Canada or imported into it. As its real merits become more widely known as a text-book for Schools and Colleges, as well as a trusty companion to the actual Accountant, its diffusion will spread more generally, year by year, until it has superseded—as it ought to do—every book of the kind extant; because it is more practical and more easily understood than any other. Its triumphs already have been very great. Many of the best Accountants in the Dominion have received their instructions from it, under the Author, Mr. W. R. ORR, of the Mercantile Academy, Toronto. It has been adopted by the Board of Public Instruction of Ontario, for use in all the Schools; and what is perhaps, of greater significance, is that it has been adopted by the Bureau of Public Instruction of the City of New York, for the use of the Schools of that commercial metropolis: and last, though not least, it has become the only text-book on this subject used in Upper Canada College.

Every typographical error in the First Edition has been corrected by the Author. A few alterations have been made by him in the text, to make it in full harmony with his General Questions, at the beginning of the work; and the Author's Arithmetical Rule has been appended, to determine the Amount of Goods on hand at the time of a fire, to the other invaluable Commercial Arithmetical Rules.

In this Edition will be found the Critiques of the Press all over Canada, from Halifax to Sarnia, and of some of the best business men in the Dominion.

To insure the most correct mode of studying for one's self, or of teaching most successfully the Dominion Accountant, the Author's Copyright Blanks should be used, which are also published by us.

A. DREDGE & CO.

Toronto, November, 1873.

CONTENTS.

	PAG
PREFACE	iii

GENERAL QUESTIONS.—Containing Definitions, Principles, Rules and Examples, wherein the use of all the Books, and the various kinds of accounts are explained agreeably to the strict Mathematical nature of the science, and the best and most modern practice, as well as the mode of proceeding with the work in every particular, from the first Entry in opening a set of books until they are balanced or closed; and the principles of Double and Single Entry discussed . ix

FIRST SET.—Containing a Cash Account only 1

SECOND " " " and Personal Accounts 11

THIRD " " " " another Real Account . . . 22

FOURTH " " " " a General Goods Account . . . 38

FIFTH " " " Examples of Personal Accounts—Exhibiting Cash and Credit transactions in addition to real accounts . . . 49

SIXTH SET.—Containing Examples of Real Accounts, sub-divided into various kinds of Goods. Also, transactions by Bills, with the Interest, Discount, etc., in which each Entry is separately Journalized 66

SEVENTH SET.—In which the transactions are Journalized collectedly, according to the usage of the best wholesale houses, with Cash Book, Bills Receivable and Payable Books, and Day Book; made up from the transactions of the Waste Book of the Sixth Set . . 110

EIGHTH SET.—Consisting of Single and Joint Consignments, Adventures, Factorships, Partnerships, etc.; comprising, in a narrow compass, the chief difficulties in Book-keeping 135

NINTH SET.—In which the Single Entry method is illustrated by changing the Fifth Set Double Entry into Single 167

	PAGE
SUBSIDIARY BOOKS.—Containing Examples of a book of House Expenses, and Cash Book, with explanations of these, as well as explanations of the nature and use of Invoice Books, Sales Book, Bills Receivable and Payable Books, etc., etc.	175
GENERAL OBSERVATIONS.	183
COMPENDIUM OF MERCHANTS' ACCOUNTS.—Containing Particular Rules for the true stating of Debtor and Creditor in all cases that can happen in the whole course of a Merchant's dealings	186
APPENDIX.—Containing Arithmetical Rules, Forms of Bills, etc., Examples of Equation of Payments or Averaging Notes, and the Converting of Sterling Money into Halifax and Decimal Currency, and *vice versa*; Exchange, Account Current, Abbreviations, Signs and Explanations of Commercial Terms or Expressions	209

INTRODUCTION.

GENERAL QUESTIONS,*
ON THE THEORY AND PRACTICE OF BOOK-KEEPING.

The Object of Book-keeping.

1. What is the object of Book-keeping?
To enable me to know at any time how my property is situated.

2. Explain this.
In business my property is continually undergoing changes; and a knowledge of Book-keeping enables me to trace my property through all these changes, and determine where, and how it is situated.

3. Give an example.
If I buy goods and pay cash, the Merchandise Account is increased and the Cash Account decreased, and *vice versa*. In like manner every transaction, whether I buy and sell for cash or on credit, affects my property, and changes it both in kind and position.

Book-keeping, and the Methods.

4. What then is Book-keeping?
It is simply a noting of the changes which occur in my property, or a systematic record of my business transactions.

5. How many methods of Book-keeping are there?
Two—Single and Double Entry.

6. Explain Single Entry.
By this method I make only *one* entry of each transaction, in the Ledger.

7. Illustrate this.
If I sell goods to A. B. on credit, I open an account for him in the Ledger, and debit his account To Merchandise, without making the contra entry.

---

* Particular Questions and Directions, the original ones, will be found in connection with each set in the body of the book; I have, nevertheless, thought these General Questions of sufficient importance to place them at the beginning of the work, that the pupil might study them thoroughly before commencing to write out the Books. I may add, that many of these questions, answers and explanations are not to be found in the original work, nor in any other treatise on Book-keeping that I know of. They are the product of my own experience—a quarter of a century's extensive practice as a Book-keeper and an Auditor of Accounts.

8. What is Double Entry?
It requires, at least, *two* entries in the Ledger for each transaction.

9. Illustrate this also.
If, as in the case above, I sell goods to A. B., I not only debit his account To Merchandise, but I also make the corresponding entry, and credit the Merchandise Account by A. B.'s.*

10. What then seems to be the real difference between the Single and Double Entry methods?
By the first method I open, in the Ledger, only the Nominal and Personal Accounts; whereas, by the latter, I open the *three* kinds of accounts, viz., the Real, the Personal, and the Nominal. (See Q. 29.)

11. Do you wish to make it appear that the opening, or not opening, of the Real Accounts in the Ledger, constitutes the principal difference between the two systems?
I do. If I have not the Real Accounts in the Ledger, I can make but *one* entry of the transaction in it; but if I open the Real Accounts, I must, of necessity, make two entries—a Debit and a Credit. (See Q. 9.)

THE PRINCIPAL BOOKS.

12. What are the Principal Books?
The Day Book, Journal and Ledger.

13. Explain the use of each.
In the Day Book—I enter the transactions of the day at length, and in order, as they occur. In the Journal are collected, at fixed periods of time, all the transactions from all the other Books, under their proper Debits and Credits. And in the Ledger, they are arranged under their respective Headings or Titles.

14. What is the infallible rule for Debiting and Crediting?
Debit *In*, Credit *Out*—*i. e.*, the thing received is debtor to the thing† given, or to the person† from whom it is received.‡

---

* The proper wording of an Entry—or what should be written in an account in the Ledger, has not always been clearly defined. The wording of every entry in every account in the Ledger should be the heading or title of another, and nothing more. If I make the Merchandise Account Debtor to Cash, *i. e.*, to the Cash Account, I must credit the Cash Account By Merchandise, *i. e.*, the Merchandise Account. Accounts are not debited and credited *to* or *by* things, viz.: Cash, Goods, etc., or persons, but by the accounts whose headings represent these things or persons. By this simple method I am enabled, when I look at an entry in one account, to tell instantly to what other account the amount has been (or should be) placed, and to which side of it, and I know, just as well as if I had been present during the sale or purchase, what changes took place in my property to cause such entry.

† Remember it is the *Account* which represents the thing or person that is debited or credited, and not the thing or person individually.

‡ This answer covers the whole ground, whether the transactions be cash or credit ones.

15. Which is the Dr. (debtor) and which is the Cr. (creditor) side of the folio in the Ledger?

The left hand side is the Dr., and the right hand side the Cr., and the Title or heading, *i. e.*, the name of the account, should be written between them, thus: Dr.————Cash————Cr.

THE SUBSIDIARY BOOKS.

16. What are the principal Subsidiary Books?

The Cash Book—Bills Receivable and Payable Books—Invoice Books (inwards and outwards)—the Warehouse Book or Stock Ledger, and the Sales Book.

17. Describe the use of each.

1st. The Cash Book.—This book, like the Ledger, has a Dr. and a Cr. side; all moneys received are entered on the Dr. side, and all paid out on the Cr. side. By this means I am enabled to keep my Cash transactions in a collected form, and to detect at any time any discrepancy that may occur between the entries in the Cash Book, and the actual cash on hand.

2nd. The Bill Books.—These books are ruled with columns to suit the Headings (see Bill Books, Sixth Set), and contain the record of my Bills Receivable and Payable, in order of Date, etc., and by referring to the columns headed "When Due" and "When Payable," I can ascertain, in a moment, on what day any particular Bill falls Due or becomes Payable. Much valuable time is thus saved to the merchant.

3rd. Invoice Books—In these books are entered, in detail, the Invoices, *i. e.* the Accounts of all goods received or sent out by me. They are of great utility as books of reference to determine quantity, quality and price. It is not necessary to enter the details in the Day Book or Journal,—the totals are sufficient—with reference to No. of Invoice.

4th. Warehouse Book.—For this book no particular form needs be prescribed, as its form must necessarily be as varied as are the products of Commerce itself. In it is entered the number of packages or the quantity of goods received into, or taken out of the warehouse; and it is a check upon the purchases and sales. The prices of the goods may or may not be entered in this book; but if entered, they will be found very serviceable at the time of taking stock.

5th. Sales Book.—This, like the Warehouse Book, must be accommodated in form to the peculiarities of the business in which it is used. It is generally kept by Wholesale Merchants, and of necessity by Commission Merchants, and is designed to show the particulars of the sales, the number, weight, or measure, and the price of the articles sold, together with all charges to which they are liable. It is sufficient to carry the totals to the Day Book or Journal.

18. Have you named all the Subsidiary Books?

No; there are others; but those above mentioned have a direct connexion with the keeping of the principal books.

19. Can you tell me anything of a little book which should be used by every one who keeps a Cash Account, but not described by any author you have read?

A Bank Pass Book, in which to enter the amounts deposited in the Bank and withdrawn from it.

20. Although you have correctly described a Bank Pass Book, do you consider the answer given a correct one, especially when you reflect that in the question asked there was nothing said about Banking; I spoke only of keeping a Cash Account?

The answer was irrelevant; I should have said a Cash Balance Memorandum Book.

21. Explain the use and importance of this much neglected little book.

Every time the Cash Account in the Cash Book is Closed or Balanced—say every day, week, fortnight, or month, as the case may be, I should enter in this book the Balance of Cash on hand, as per Cash Book; and then, every day, before leaving the office, I should, by adding up the Dr. side of the Cash Book, ascertain the amount received during the day, and add it to the balance entered in the Cash Balance Book. I should then add up the Cr. side to ascertain the amount paid out, and deduct it from the sum already found; this difference will agree with the amount of the cash on hand, (which is found by counting it) if the Cash Book has been correctly kept, and be again the balance for the next day. As the Cash on hand is the only certain check upon the entries in the Cash Book, the importance of this practice must be obvious; and as some such method as the above is absolutely necessary in keeping a Cash Account, no one should be entrusted with its management who is ignorant of the principle involved in this simple method of testing the correctness of the Cash Account, or too negligent or too apathetic to rigorously apply it.*

TRANSFERRING THE ENTRIES.

22. Now, that you have described the Books, how do you proceed to transfer the entries from the one to the other?

In every case, the page or folio of the book from which the entry is taken should be written opposite the entry in the book to which it is taken; and the page or folio of the book, into which it has been transferred, should be placed opposite the entry in the book from which it was taken. Thus making a complete reference, forwards and backwards, to each entry throughout the books.

---

* If employers would give their attention to this matter, and see to its being enforced, some of the temptation, at least, would be removed out of the way of those in charge of cash. I know, from experience, that the Cash Account is too frequently balanced by the difference between the two sides, without ascertaining that this difference agrees with the Cash on hand, which is *the Balance*. No practice is more reprehensible than this, or so likely to lead to disastrous results.

THE TRIAL BALANCE.

23. What steps do you take to insure the correctness of the transfer?

When I have transferred the entries, usually at stated periods, from one book to another, as above described, I turn back to the beginning and compare the entries thus transferred, one by one, and item by item, with the original ones, placing the check mark (√) opposite the amounts in both the books, till all are thus marked and found correct.

Correct checking, both as regards names and amounts, is of the utmost importance.

24. When all the entries have been carried in this way to their respective accounts in the Ledger, and carefully checked, what other precaution is taken to prove that the Ledger has been correctly posted?

A Trial Balance is made out.

25. What is a Trial Balance?

The Trial Balance Sheet or Book has Dr. and Cr. columns* similar to a Ledger folio. I now proceed to add up, in pencil, all the accounts in the Ledger, placing the sum of the amounts of the Dr. side of each account in the Dr. columns of the Balance Sheet, and the sum of the amounts of the Cr. side in the Cr. columns of the Sheet. I then add up the amounts thus collected in the Dr. and Cr. columns of the Balance Sheet, to ascertain if they be equal, as they ought to be, if the Ledger has been correctly posted.

That these totals should be equal, is manifest from the principle of Double Entry, viz : That every Dr. has a Cr., and every Cr. a Dr., *i. e.*, an equal amount placed to the opposite sides of the corresponding accounts ; consequently the sum of all the Debits must equal the sum of all the Credits.

26. Is the Trial Balance, then, an infallible proof that the accounts in the Ledger are correct, when the two columns show equal amounts?

It is not. Every entry in every account in the Ledger might be reversed, *i. e.*, placed to the opposite sides of the accounts, and every account might contain the entries of any other account but its own, and still the result of the Trial Balance would be the same.

27. Is not the Trial Balance, consequently, useless?

No. If the person keeping the books thoroughly understands the grand principles of Dr. and Cr. by Double Entry, and be careful in checking his books, the Trial Balance will then be the most satisfactory proof that can be obtained of the correctness of the posting, previous to making the Final Balance.

---

* These columns are placed differently, according to fancy, sometimes to the right and left of the folio, with the names of the accounts between them [See Trial Balance, Second Set, page 17] and sometimes with both Dr. and Cr. columns to the right, like a Journal.

The Different Kinds of Accounts.

28. How many kinds of Accounts are there?
Only three.

29. Name them.
(1.) Real. (2.) Personal, and (3.) Fictitious—Nominal, or Accommodating.

30. What are Real Accounts?
They are the names of the Accounts which represent my property: such as Cash, Merchandise, Bills Receivable, Bank, Bank Stock, etc.—in fact, whatever can be realized upon and turned into money, are called Real Accounts.

1. BILLS PAYABLE.—This account is placed, by all the authors that I have read upon the subject, among Real Accounts. They are clearly wrong. A Real Account is an account of property which can be exchanged for money, or bartered, *i. e.*, realized upon. The Bills Payable Account differs in its *nature* from Real Accounts. *How can I realize upon my liabilities or debts?* Again, Real Accounts are closed *By* Balance; Bills Payable Account always *To* Balance; thus differing also from the Real Accounts in the mode of its Bal. In this respect it likewise differs from the Personal and Accommodating Accounts (See questions 31 and 32). It is therefore an anomaly in accounts, and the only definition which I can give of it is, that it is an aggregate account of my indebtedness to persons, transferred from their respective accounts to it, by my acceptance of their Bills or Notes of Hand.

2. Bank Stock and Bank Deposit Accounts are Real Accounts, whereas a Bank Current Account must be considered a Personal Account.

31. What are Personal Accounts?
The Accounts which represent the persons with whom I do business on *Credit*.*

32. What are the Fictitious, Nominal or Accommodating Accounts?
These Accounts represent myself—the merchant—and are designated Stock, Profit and Loss, and Balance.

33. Why do you say these Accounts represent the Merchant?
Because the Stock, etc., stands for his name.

34. Suppose there were partners in the firm, would one Stock Account be sufficient?
No. I would then be obliged to open a Stock Account for each of the partners, thus: A. B.'s Stock Account, C. B.'s Stock Account, etc.†

---

* The answer to this question, in every work I have read on Book-keeping, is erroneous, and calculated to mislead the learner. The answer invariably given is, "The Accounts of persons with whom I do business." Nothing can be more absurd. If I have *Cash* transactions with a thousand persons, amounting to millions of money, I open no account for these persons in the Ledger, because they paid for what they got, and I paid them for what I purchased. It is plain, therefore, Personal Accounts are opened for those only *who deal on Credit*.

† Balancing the Books in this case does not affect the Company's Stock or Capital Account; it remains just as it was. See page 139.

Order of Opening Accounts.

35. Can you tell the order of time in which these accounts should be opened in the Ledger?

The Stock Account is to be opened first, and, as I have already said, it represents myself, *i. e.*, in it are entered, on the Cr. side, all I possess in the business, and on the Dr. all I owe. It shows my position, commercially, at the commencement of my business, as clearly as a good mirror reflects me physically. If I look into the Stock Account, I see on my left hand, or Dr. side, all I owe, and on the Cr., or right hand side, all I possess. The difference, of course, would be my net estate.

The Profit and Loss Account is opened when any casual gain or loss requires to be entered in the corresponding accounts; and at the time of closing the books, the results of all its branches, viz: Interest, Discount, Expense, Wages, Commission Account, etc., are brought into it, as well as the gain or loss on the Merchandize Account, etc.

The Balance Account is opened when I commence to close the accounts in the Ledger, and all the balances of all the accounts are brought into it. Instead of opening this account in the ordinary Ledger, it is often kept in a separate book, called the Balance Ledger.

Of the Balance—Real Accounts.

36. How are Real Accounts closed or balanced?

They are all closed—first, *By* Balance for the amount on hand, if there be any; and—second, *To* or *By* Profit and Loss for the gain or loss.

37. Why did you not say *To* or *By* Balance, instead of *By* only, in closing Real Accounts?

Because, in the case of the Cash Account, I cannot pay out more than I receive; also, in the Merchandize Account, I cannot sell a greater quantity or number of packages of goods than was bought; and as what came in was entered on the Dr. side of the respective accounts, and the amounts paid out in the one, and the quantity or number sold in the other, were entered on the Cr. side, it is impossible that the Cr. side in either account can exceed the Dr. And as the Balance in all cases is taken to the less side to make both equal, it can never be carried to the Dr. side, because that can never be the less, but always the greater, while any portion of my property remains on hand, unpaid out, or unsold.*

38. Are all the Real Accounts closed, as you have said, To or By Profit and Loss?

Two of them are never closed To or By Profit and Loss, viz., the Cash and Bills Receivable Accounts.

---

* When there is no Balance, *i. e.*, when all is sold, the Accounts are closed To or By Profit and Loss only

39. Why?

Because in receiving or paying out Cash, it neither increases nor decreases in value, *i. e.*, if I receive five dollars, all I can possibly pay out are five dollars; and if I pay out only four, I must account for the other dollar, which is the Balance, and will close the account.

40. But suppose, as in the case above, you find, on counting the Cash on hand, that you have only ninety cents instead of a dollar, how are you to close the account?

I must first use all diligence to find out the error, and if I fail in this I may charge the ten cents to myself, or to Profit and Loss, and thus adjust the account; so that the ninety cents, the Balance on hand, will then close it.

41. You have said the Cash and Bills Receivable Accounts can never be closed To or By Profit and Loss; have you not used it as a closing entry just now?

I have not. It was only used as an adjusting entry; and whether I closed the Cash Account at the time the error was discovered or not, it was proper to make such entry, so that the Cash Book entries and the actual Cash on hand might correspond. It would not have been a closing entry, had I continued to make further records in the Cash Book; no more would it have been, had I at once balanced the account. In the case above referred to, you will have observed the Balance entry comes last, whereas, in the other Real Accounts—as Merchandize—it is entered first, and Profit and Loss last, which must ever be the practice, or the gain or loss could not be ascertained at all. The Cash Account can never, therefore, be closed either To Balance, or To or By Profit and Loss, but only By Balance for the amount on hand, if there be any. Indeed, the idea of Profit and Loss should never be entertained in connection, either with keeping a Cash Account or closing it. When all the Cash has been paid away, the two sides of the account should be equal, and the account may then be said to close itself.

42. What about the Bills Receivable Account?

It is closed similarly to the Cash Account, and the same line of argument will apply equally to it.

43. But suppose you discount the notes at the Bank, you would, of course, get less cash for them, by the amount of the discount, than their face value, and when placed to the Credit of the Bills Receivable Account, would not correspond with the amount of the notes as entered on the Dr. side of that Account.

Discount—another term for Profit and Loss—would, in this case, be used as the adjusting entry; and the cash received for the notes, together with the discount, would be equal to the face amount of the notes, and might be entered to the Cr. of the account, either separately, or jointly, By Sundries.

44. Is there not another method, in very general use, of entering the amount of the notes discounted to the Cr. of the Bills Receivable Account?

There is another mode, viz. : Enter on the Cr. side of the Bills Receivable Account the whole amount as written on the Bills—By Cash, and Dr. the Cash Account also with the full amount, To Bills Receivable; and then Cr. the Cash Account—By Discount for the amount charged by the Bank for discounting the notes. The result in both cases will be the same.

If a portion only of the notes be discounted, the amount of those remaining on hand will close or balance the account.

PERSONAL ACCOUNTS.

45. How are the Personal Accounts closed?

They are closed either *To*, or *By* Balance for the difference between the two sides.

46. How does it happen that Personal Accounts are closed To, or By Balance?

Because the persons represented by these accounts may either owe me or I may owe them. If the former, the Dr. side of the account would be the greater, and must be closed By Balance; whereas, in the latter, the Cr. side would be the greater, and must de closed To Balance.

47. Suppose you were to sell goods to some one on credit, whose ability or willingness to pay, you had no reason, at the time, to doubt, but afterwards found that he was both unable and unwilling to pay anything; how would you close the account?

By Profit and Loss for the amount at the Dr. Side, and carry it to the Profit and Loss Account.

48. Again, suppose a case similar to the last, but with this difference, you know the person to be strictly honest, and that he will pay you when he obtains the means; how would you close his account?

By the Suspense Account, to await the result.

49. Would you consider the amounts as losses in both these cases?

Only in the former. The latter amount is merely suspended, *i. e.* hung up.

The Fictitious, Nominal or Accommodating Accounts.

50. Now that you have closed the Real and Personal Accounts, and the branches of the Profit and Loss Account, what accounts yet

remain to be closed that your books may be balanced, and the state of your affairs fully known to you?

The Three Accommodating Accounts, which are closed in the following order, viz., 1st. Profit and Loss; 2nd. Balance, and 3rd. Stock.

51. *How are they closed?*

They will close each other, if the books have been correctly kept.

52. *Explain the process.*

I first add up the two sides of the Profit and Loss Account, to ascertain which is the greater; having found this, I close it To Stock for gain, if the Cr. side is the greater, and carry the amount to the Cr. side of the Stock Account—writing By Profit and Loss for gain; and if the Dr. side is the greater, By Stock for loss, and carry this amount to the Dr. side of the Stock Account—writing To Profit and Loss for loss.* I next close the Balance Account By Stock for the difference between the two sides, which is my Net Estate, or the Excess of Assets over Liabilities, and carry this amount likewise to the Stock Account—writing To Balance for Net Estate. The two sides of the Stock Account, if the books have been correctly kept, must now be equal, and the books closed.

53. *Can you demonstrate the last statement to be correct, viz., that the two sides of the Stock Account must be equal, whether you have gained or lost, if the books have been correctly kept?*

I shall endeavour to do so. If, as has been stated, the gain found in the Profit and Loss Account was carried to the Cr. side of the Stock Account and added to what I possessed when I began business, (See Q. 35) the sum of these two items would be equal to what I possess now, because I can only be worth what I had at first and what I have gained; and as the Balance Account shows, on the Dr. side all my assets, and the Cr. side all my liabilities, then the difference between the two sides of this account must be my Net Estate, or what I am actually worth at the present moment; and as we have seen that the Balance Account is closed By Stock for this amount, and the Stock Account Dr. with it, To Balance, what I possess now is by this means placed in the Stock Account, opposite what I had when I commenced business, together with what I have since gained, and these sums must be equal, if the books have been correctly kept, as they both represent the same thing, viz., what I am actually worth at present. Again, if I have lost, it is clear I cannot have as much now as when I began, and it will be found that the Dr. side of the Profit and Loss Account is greater than the Cr., and will therefore be closed By Stock, and the amount brought to the Dr. side of the Stock Account, To Profit and Loss for loss; to which will be

---

* By noticing the expressions used in closing the Profit and Loss Account, the pupil may deduce the following, viz: If the business has produced a gain, since the books were last balanced, or since they were first opened, the Cr. side of the Profit and Loss Account will be the greater; and if a loss has been the result, the Dr. side will be the greater. An unerring rule for making entries in the Profit and Loss Account, is, enter the losses on the Dr. side, and the gains on the Cr. side.

I would here remind the pupil that, in closing the books when kept by Double Entry, every Dr. must have a corresponding Cr., and every Cr. a corresponding Dr., just as in posting the Ledger.

added my diminished capital, because, as before, the Balance Account is closed By Stock, and the amount carried to the Dr. side of the Stock Account, and added to the loss; and as the loss and what I now possess must be equal to what I began with, which is at the Cr. side of the Stock Account, both sides of the account must now be equal, as well as when there is a gain.

54. Can you state the substance of this more briefly?

I shall try. If, in the Stock Account, I add what I possess now to what I owed when I began (which is on the Dr. side of Stock), and what I now owe, to what I possessed when I began (which is on the Cr. side of Stock), the difference of these two sums will be equal to the difference between the two sides of the Profit and Loss Account, *i. e.*, the difference between the two sides of the Profit and Loss Account, whether a gain or loss, added to the smaller of these two sums in the Stock Account, will make the two sides equal and close the books.*

55. Is your Ledger now in a proper state to receive the Entries which have accumulated in the Day Book and Primary books, during the time you were occupied in balancing it?

The balances used in closing the accounts have yet to be brought down, before the Ledger is in a fit state to receive further entries.

56. To which side of the accounts do you bring down the balances?

To the opposite side, *i. e.*, if I find them on the Dr. side, I bring them down to the Cr. side, and *vice versa*. This operation re-opens the accounts in the Ledger, and prepares it for receiving entries until the time of making the next balance.

WM. R. ORR.

Toronto, 1st June, 1868.

---

* The reason the words To or By Stock are used, in closing the Profit and Loss and Balance Accounts, is, that the difference between the two sides of these two accounts—the one representing the gain or loss, and the other my Net Estate, at the time of balancing the books, may be brought into the Stock Account; and that what I now possess, viz., the amount carried from the Balance Account, may be brought down to the Credit side of the Stock Account, when the balances of the other accounts are brought down, and the books re-opened.

It may be remarked that the differences between the two sides of any two of these accounts will close the third. Thus, the Balance and Stock Accounts will close the Profit and Loss Account, and the Stock and Profit and Loss Accounts will close the Balance Account; and we have seen already that the differences between the two sides of the Profit and Loss and Balance Accounts closed the Stock Account, and proved the correctness of the books.

ELEMENTS OF BOOK-KEEPING.

FIRST SET.

CASH ACCOUNT.

As keeping an account of money received and paid, furnishes the simplest example of Book-keeping, we commence with a Cash Account.

Let us suppose a person engaged in money transactions, of receiving and paying, which are written down as they occur; it is obvious that, if he wish to know what money he ought to have on hand, he must pick out all the sums received, and add them together, and also all the sums paid; and then, by subtracting the one from the other, he will be able to tell what money he should have on hand (if any); and afterwards, by comparing the sums thus indicated in his book, with what he actually has in his desk or elsewhere, he can tell whether he has kept his books correctly.

Now, in order to be able to do this at any time, without the delay of separating the sums received, from those paid, the method adopted in Book-keeping is, to have a Cash Account, either in a book by itself, or in a book among other accounts.

For this purpose, take the two opposite pages of a book (which two pages taken together are then called a folio); rule each with money columns towards the right hand, and a column for the date on the left hand. Then write on the top of the left hand page, in a text hand, "CASH, DR.," and on the right hand page, "CONTRA, CR.;" the former is then called the Dr. or debtor side, the latter Cr. or credit side.*

---

* Sometimes one broad page is made to hold both the Dr. and Cr. side. Arranging accounts in the manner described above, on two opposite pages, the one for whatever comes in, called the Dr. side, the other for what goes out, called the Cr. side, is what is meant by keeping books by Debtor and Creditor.

Elements of Book-keeping.

All sums on hand or received, are entered on the Dr. side; and all sums paid, on the Cr. side; because the word *Cash*, at the top of the page, is put for the person himself to whom the books belong, in so far as cash is concerned; and, in Book-keeping, every one is considered Dr. for what he receives, and Cr. by what he gives out.

DIRECTIONS.

The first thing that the pupil should do, is to copy out, in a fair legible hand, the transactions stated from page 4 to 7, into a book ruled with money columns towards the right, and a column for the date towards the left, and either with or without a head line. This book is called, sometimes, the Waste Book, because the entries in it have been regarded as superseded and rendered no longer necessary, by being transferred to the Journal (a book afterwards to be described), and it is sometimes called the Day Book, because the transactions are entered in it every day, as they occur, without technicality of form.

Let him then open an account for Cash, as above directed; and having done so, let him go over, *seriatim*, the transactions which he has copied into his Waste Book, carefully observing in each, whether the cash was received or paid out, entering as he proceeds, whatever was received on the Dr. or left hand side, and what was paid out on the Cr. or right hand side, in this form:

First Set—Directions.

1868.		CASH.	DR.	1868.		CONTRA.	CR.
			$ c.				$ c.
Jan.	1	To Bal. on hand..	400 00	Jan.	1	By John Jones....	325 50
,,	2	,, Sales	85 70	,,	2	,, Expenses.....	68 75
,,	2	,, W. Thompson	165 50	,,	3	,, Balance......	256 95
			$651 20				$651 20

Having thus entered all the different sums on their respective sides, let the pupil then add up, first, the one side, and then the other; let him then subtract the smaller sum from the larger, and at the bottom of the smaller side let him enter the difference by which they will be made equal. This is called balancing an account, that is, bringing both sides to an equality, like a pair of balances equally poised; and the sum necessary to bring them to an equality is called the balance, and entered To* or By Balance, according as it is required on the Dr. or Cr. side of the account.

Thus, in the above example, the Dr. side was first added up, making $651.20; then the Cr. side was added up, and was found to be $394.25; this being subtracted from $651.20, leaves $256.95, which is added to the Cr. side, with the words By Balance, before it, and thus makes both sides equal. $256.95, therefore, is the money on hand, and ought to correspond to the money actually in the possession of the person whose transactions are recorded.

---

* NOTE.—"To Balance" can never occur in balancing Cash (or any other real account), as you cannot pay out more than you receive, consequently the Cr. side can never be the greater.

W. R. ORR.

4 WASTE BOOK.

The tranactions in this set are to be regarded merely as the items or transactions of a Cash Account, and all that the pupil is expected to do, is to distinguish Cash received from Cash given out, that he may enter the former on the Dr. side of the Cash Account, and the latter on the Cr. side.

TORONTO, 1st JANUARY, 1868.

L.F.		$	C.
1	I have on hand at this date, Cash	500	00
	This is the balance on hand from the former time of balancing the Cash, and must be entered on the Dr. side of the Cash Account, with the date and words, To balance on hand* before it.		
	——————— 1 ———————		
1	Paid John Cummings, for Books, as per invoice .	360	75
	This is money paid, and therefore must be entered on the Cr. side, By John Cummings.		
	——————— 1 ———————		
1	Sales this day	89	25
	Sales are what I sell, and, therefore, the money is received, and goes to the Dr. side, To Sales. (Should be, To Goods for Sales —W. R. ORR.		
	——————— 2 ———————		
1	House expenses for last week	8	40
	House expenses imply money going out, and therefore this sum goes to the Cr. side : By House Expenses.		

* NOTE.—"Balance on hand," that is, the amount of Cash actually in possession at the time of the former balance.
         W. R. ORR.

FIRST SET.

TORONTO, 2ND JANUARY, 1868.

L.F.		$	C.
1	Received from William Thompson, for an Encyclopædia sold him	200	00
	——————— 2 ———————		
1	Received for sales this day	48	50
	——————— 3 ———————		
1	Paid Houston & Co., for 100 copies Euclid's Elements	125	00
	——————— 3 ———————		
1	Paid House Rent, one half year, ending 25th December last...................... Enter this, By Expenses.	100	00
	——————— 3 ———————		
1	Paid Taxes, Grand Jury Cess. for Michaelmas Term .... Enter this, By Expenses.	19	25
	——————— 3 ———————		
1	Received from John Hunter, Rent for Stable, one half year, to 25th December..........	47	50
	——————— 3 ———————		
1	Received for sales this day................	67	40
	——————— 4 ———————		
1	Paid Thomas Mason his account for painting house	27	50
	——————— 5 ———————		
1	Paid John Cummings, for Books, as per invoice	136	40

BOOK-KEEPING.

TORONTO, 5TH JANUARY, 1868.

L.F.		$	C.
1	Paid Thomas White his account for printing Catechism	48	00
	——————— 5 ———————		
1	Received for sales this day.................	120	68
	——————— 6 ———————		
1	Received Legacy from the Executors of the late Mrs. Mary Campbell, deducting duty and other expenses...............................	470	00
	This cash came in and nothing went out, therefore, Cash Dr. To Profit and Loss—not to Legacy.		
	——————— 6 ———————		
1	Paid wages to Shopman, due 28th ult..........	38	50
	Enter, By Wages or Expenses.		
	——————— 6 ———————		
1	Paid Patterson for Coals, 2 tons	15	00
	Enter this By Expenses.		
	——————— 6 ———————		
1	Paid William Wilson his account for Book-binding	47	50
	——————— 6 ———————		
1	Received for this day's sales.................	97	45
	——————— 7 ———————		
1	Remitted Waddell & Co., on account of Books purchased	175	75
	To Remit, is to send money to a distance. This, therefore, is Cash going out, and goes to the Cr. side of the Cash Account.		
	——————— 7 ———————		
1	Received from Samuel Ely, for Books furnished to Ross library	22	25

FIRST SET.

TORONTO, 7TH JANUARY, 1868.

L.F.		$	C.
1	Paid Hanny his account for repairs of Shop and House	65	50
	——————— 7 ———————		
1	Received from Hanny, for old shop furnishings, including glass-case.......................	20	00
	——————— 7 ———————		
1	Received for sales this day	54	75

The cash on hand to close this account is $570.23. This amount agrees with the difference of the two sides, which proves the account correct, and will close it.

W. R. ORR.

The pupil should be made to do this exercise upon a separate piece of paper, properly ruled, before he enter it in his book; and he should not be permitted to leave it till he fully understand it.

The teacher should also dictate to him other transactions, and require him to post them, that he may acquire readiness in placing cash going out, and cash coming in, to the proper sides of the Cash Account.

QUESTIONS ON THE FIRST SET.

What is meant by Cash? Why is this book begun with a Cash Account? If you wrote down in a book the money you received and the money you gave out, in the order in which the transactions occurred, what would you need to do that you might ascertain whether your accounts were correct or not? What plan is adopted to avoid this tedious operation? In what kind of book would you require to keep your Cash Account? What is a folio in the language of Book-keeping? What would you write on the left hand page of your folio? What on the right? Suppose you receive a sum of money, on which side would you place it? Why? What does the word Cash stand for?

BOOK-KEEPING.

QUESTIONS ON THE FIRST SET—Continued.

What is the difference of Dr. and Cr. ? What is the first thing that the pupil ought to do? What is this book called? In what order do you enter your transactions in this book? After having written out the Waste Book, what is to be done? What is to be carefully observed? On what side do you enter Sales, House Expenses? When the sums are all entered, what is to be done? When is the balance entered To* and when By? Why, in the example given here, is the Balance added to the Creditor side? What is meant by remitting money?

---

* In Cash never to Balance—(See General Questions 36 and 37).

W. B. ORR.

FIRST SET.

CASH ACCOUNT.

First Set—Cash Account.

FOL. 1 — Dr. — Cash — Cr. — FOL. 1

		Dr.	P.D.B.	$	C.			Cr.	P.D.B.	$	C.
1868						1868					
Jan.	1	To Balance	4	500	00	Jan.	1	By J. Cummings.	4	360	75
,,	,,	,, Goods (sales)	,,	89	25	,,	,,	,, Expenses....	,,	8	40
,,	2	,, W. Thompson	5	200	00	,,	3	,, Houston & Co	5	125	00
,,	,,	,, Goods (sales)	,,	48	50	,,	,,	,, Expenses....	,,	100	00
,,	3	,, J. Hunter ..	,,	47	50	,,	,,	,, Do.	,,	19	25
,,	,,	,, Goods (sales)	,,	67	40	,,	4	,, Thos. Mason.	,,	27	50
,,	5	,, Do. do,	6	120	68	,,	5	,, J. Cummings.	,,	136	40
,,	6	,, Profit & Loss.	,,	470	00	,,	,,	,, Thos. White.	6	48	00
,,	,,	,, Goods (sales)	,,	97	45	,,	6	,, Expenses....	,,	38	50
,,	7	,, Samuel Ely..	,,	22	25	,,	,,	,, Do.	,,	15	00
,,	,,	,, Hanny......	7	20	00	,,	,,	,, Wm. Wilson.	,,	47	50
,,	,,	,, Goods (sales)	,,	54	75	,,	7	,, Waddell & Co	,,	175	75
						,,	,,	,, Hanny......	7	65	50
						,,	,,	,, Balance......		570	23
				1737	78					1737	78
	8	To Balance		570	23						

* P.D.B.—Page Day Book.

BOOK-KEEPING.

SECOND SET.

CASH AND PERSONAL ACCOUNTS.

If I have transactions in money with other persons, such as paying and receiving, borrowing and lending, etc., it is necessary not only to keep an account of my Cash, that I may know at any time what I have received, what given out, and how much I have on hand; but also to keep an account with each of the persons with whom I have dealings; that I may know whether I owe anything to them, and how much; whether they owe anything to me, and how much; or whether our accounts be clear.

In order to effect this purpose, I first open a Cash Account, as directed in the First Set, which is to be my own account; the word "CASH," at the top, standing, as before, for myself, in regard to Cash.

I then open an account for each of the persons with whom I have dealings, that is, I write each of their names upon a folio of the Ledger, putting Dr. (debtor) on the left hand page, and Cr. (creditor) on the right.

When I receive money from any of these persons, I put down on the Dr., on left hand side of the Cash Account, "To" that person, adding the sum in the money column, because I am considered debtor to the person for what he gives me. I then turn to that person's account, and upon the Cr., or right hand side, I write, "By Cash," adding the same sum, because that person paid it out, and therefore he is Cr. for it. The same sum, therefore, will appear on the Dr. side of the Cash, that is, of my account, and on the Cr. side of his account; intimating that, apart from all other dealings, I am his debtor, and he is my creditor for that sum.

But if I pay him money, I turn to the Dr., or left hand side of his account, and write, "To Cash," adding the sum, because he received it, and therefore is debtor for it; and then I turn to the Cr., or right hand side of the Cash, that is, my own account, and write, "By" that person, adding the sum; so that this sum will appear on the Cr. side of my account, and on the Dr. side of his; intimating that I am his creditor, and that he is my debtor for that sum. This system of entering all transactions twice, namely, on the Dr. side of one account, and on the Cr. side of another, is called Book-keeping by *double entry*. It proceeds upon the obvious principle that every debtor must have a creditor, and every creditor a debtor; and it keeps an account both for the debtor and the creditor in every transaction. Whatever, therefore, is entered on the Dr. side of one account, is entered on the Cr. side of another, and *vice versa*.

Having gone over all the items in the following Waste Book in this way, I add up all the items on the Dr. sides of all the accounts into one sum, and also all the items on the Cr. side into another, to ascertain whether they be equal, as they ought to be, if they have been posted correctly. This is called a Trial Balance. Having found, or made them correct, I then balance the Cash Account as before, which will show me how much money I have on hand. In the same way I balance the accounts kept with different persons, which will show me how much I owe to any of them, or how much any of them owes to me.

SECOND SET.

WASTE BOOK.

The transactions in this set are mere cash transactions, *i. e.*, giving out and receiving money; but they are cash transactions on credit, and therefore accounts with those persons who give or receive credit, are necessary.

TORONTO, 1st JANUARY, 1868.

L.F.		$	C.
1 1	I have on hand, commencing business, Cash....	250	00
	This Cash on hand must be put, as before, on the Dr. side of the Cash Account; but for a reason, to be afterwards explained, the words "To Stock," and not "To Balance," must be written before it.		
1 1	Borrowed of William Reid	100	06
	This money came in, therefore it must go to the Dr. side of my account, *i. e.*, the Cash Account; but it went out from William Reid, and therefore it must be entered on the Cr. side of his account.		
1 2	Paid James Thompson......................	265	80
	This money being paid, goes to the Cr. side of my Cash Account, but to the Dr. side of James Thompson's account, because he received it.		
1 2	Received from John Robertson	100	00

SECOND SET.

TORONTO, 3RD JANUARY, 1868.

L.F.		$	C.
1	Received from James Thompson	345	75
2	——————— 4 ———————		
1	Paid William Reid, money borrowed	100	00
1	——————— 5 ———————		
1	Lent John Robertson	175	10
2	——————— 5 ———————		
1*	Paid William Reid	135	50
1	——————— 6 ———————		
1	Lent William Reid	50	00
1	——————— 8 ———————		
1	Received from John Robertson	125	00
2	——————— 8 ———————		
1	Paid James Thompson	186	10
2	——————— 9 ———————		
1	Received from John Tod, for James Thompson..	38	20
2	Here the cash comes in; it is therefore entered on the Dr. side of the Cash Account, "To James Thompson," and as it came on account of James Thompson, on the Cr. side of his account; and no account is necessary for John Tod.		
	——————— 10 ———————		
1	Advanced for John Robertson................	77	50
2	Here I paid cash for John Robertson; the sum, therefore, goes to the Cr. side of the Cash Account, "By John Robertson," but to the Dr. side of his account, because the cash was paid for him.		
	——————— 12 ———————		
1	John Robertson paid me the balance of his account*	27	60
2			
	——————— 14 ———————		
1	Received from James Thompson	250	00
2			

* As Robertson has paid me the balance of his account, it should therefore be closed at once, so as not to mix up the past transactions, thus closed, with future ones.

W. R. ORR.

SECOND SET.

DIRECTIONS.

When these items are posted and balanced, it will be found that I have a balance of cash on hand of $246.55; that William Reid owes me $185.50; that I owe James Thompson $182.05, and that my account with John Robertson is clear.

If I wish to know whether I am a gainer or loser on the whole, so far as these receipts and payments are concerned, it is obvious that I must add the cash that I have on hand to that which William Reid owes me, and then subtract that which I owe to James Thompson, by which it will appear that I am now possessed of $250; precisely the same sum that I had on hand on commencing the transactions.

Now the manner in which this result will be shown in a Ledger, is as follows :—If I intend at the time of opening these accounts, thus to balance and close all the accounts, I must begin with opening an account in the Ledger for Stock, writing on the top, Dr. Stock, | Contra Cr., and on the Cr. or right hand side, I must enter the cash that I had on hand at the commencement, namely, $250, writing before it the date, January 1st, and " By Cash."*

This stands, without addition or alteration, till the accounts are to be closed. Having balanced the different accounts as directed above, I open another account, for Balance, and on the left or Dr. side of that account I enter those balances that appear on the Cr. or right hand page, namely, the balance of the cash and of William Reid's account; and on the right or Cr. side, I enter those balances that appear on the Dr. or left hand page, namely, in this case, that of James Thompson. I then balance this Balance Account, *i. e.*, add up the two sides separately, and subtract the least from the greatest, and add the difference, which will be found in this case to

---

* The master may here make the pupil open a Stock Acccunt, as directed, informing him that, in practice, this is done at the commencement, but was postponed till he should be able to understand the use of it.

W. R. ORR.

be $250, to the smallest side, to make it equal with the other, writing before it, "By Stock," for my net estate. I then turn to the Stock Account, and write on the Dr. side, "To Balance," for my net estate; and as this is precisely equal to the cash entered on the other side when I began, it shows that I have neither lost nor gained, having precisely the same value of property. There is one difference, however, in my affairs, namely, that when I began I had $250 in cash, whereas I have, in closing, only $246.55; but the difference between what William Reid owes me, and what I owe James Thompson, makes up the deficiency of cash, namely, $3.45. Instead, therefore, of having $250 in cash, I have in cash $246.55, together with $3.45 owing to me more than I owe, which amounts to the same sum.

Example of the Balance Account.

Dr.	Balance.	$	c.			Contra.	$	c.
1868.				1868.				
Jan'y.	14 To Cash	246	55	Jan'y.	14	By Jas. Thompson.	182	05
,,	,, ,, Wm. Reid	185	50	,,	,,	,, Stock	250	00
		432	05				432	05

The master will make the pupil complete the balance, as here exemplified.

Form of Trial Balance.

(See Ledger Accounts, Second Set.)

	Dr.	Cr.
Stock	00 00	250 00
Cash	1236 55	990 00
William Reid	285 50	100 00
James Thompson	451 90	633 95
$	1973 95	1973 95

QUESTIONS ON THE SECOND SET.

When you have transactions in money with other persons, what is necessary besides keeping a Cash Account? Why is this necessary? How would you manage this? Would you write the names of the persons with whom you have dealings on both sides of the Ledger? On which side would you put Cr.? If you receive money, in which account would you enter it, and on which side? After you have entered it in the Cash Account, where would you enter it next? On which side? Why? Where will the sum now appear in your books? What would you understand by the position of this sum in your books, considering it apart from all other transactions you may have with the same person? Suppose now, that instead of receiving, you pay money to the same person, how would you enter it in your books? When you thus enter every transaction twice, what is this mode of Bock-keeping called? Upon what obvious principle does it proceed? If you enter in the Cr. side of one account, on which side do you enter the same sum in the other account? When you have gone over the Waste Book in this way, what are you to do? When you borrow money, on which side of your account would you enter it? What do you mean by *posting*? When you have posted all the accounts, what is your next operation? What does the Trial Balance ascertain? Why should the sums of all the debits and of

Questions on the Second Set.

all the credits be equal? If you wish to know whether you are a gainer or a loser, what would you do? When you open an account for stock in the Ledger, on which side would you enter the cash that you have on hand? When you have balanced the different accounts, what next? When this Balance Account is finished, what are you to do with it? When, in adding up the two sides, you find one greater than the other, what are you to do with the difference?

SECOND SET.

CASH AND PERSONAL ACCOUNTS.

Second Set—Ledger.

FOL. 1

DR.			STOCK.					CR.	FOL. 1	
1868.			L.F.	$	C.	1868.			P D B	$	C.
Jan.	14	To Balance ..	2	250	00	Jan.	1	By Cash......	13	250	00
						Jan.	15	By Balance ..		250	00

DR.						CASH.				CR.	
1868.			P D B	$	C.	1868.			P D B	$	C.
Jan.	1	To Stock	13	250	00	Jan.	1	By J. Thompson	13	265	80
,,	,,	,, Wm. Reid..	,,	100	00	,,	4	,, Wm. Reid..	14	100	00
,,	,,	,, J. Robertson	,,	100	00	,,	5	,, J. Robertson	,,	175	10
,,	3	,, J. Thompson	14	345	75	,,	,,	,, Wm. Reid..	,,	135	50
,,	8	,, J. Robertson	,,	125	00	,,	6	,, Wm. Reid..	,,	50	00
,,	9	,, J. Thompson	,,	38	20	,,	8	,, J. Thompson	,,	186	10
,,	12	,, J. Robertson	,,	27	60	,,	10	,, J. Robertson	,,	77	50
,,	14	,, J. Thompson	,,	250	00	,,	14	,, Balance....	L.F. 2	246	55
				1236	55					1236	55
,,	15	To Balance ..		246	55						

DR.						WM. REID.				CR.	
1868.			P D B	$	C.	1868.			P D B	$	C.
Jan.	4	To Cash......	14	100	00	Jan.	1	By Cash......	13	100	00
,,	5	,, do.	,,	135	50	,,	14	,, Balance ..	L.F. 2	185	50
,,	6	,, do.	,,	50	00						
				285	50					285	50
,,	15	To Balance ..		185	50						

Second Set—Ledger.

DR. JAS. THOMPSON. CR.

1868.			PDB	$	C.	1868.			PDB	$	C.
Jan.	1	To Cash......	13	265	80	Jan.	3	By Cash......	14	345	75
,,	8	,, do.	14	186	10	,,	9	,, do.	,,	38	20
			L.F.			,,	14	,, do.	,,	250	00
,,	14	,, Balance ..	2	182	05						
				633	95					633	95
						,,	15	By Balance ..		182	05

DR. JNO. ROBERTSON.* CR.

1868.			PDB	$	C.	1868.			PDB	$	C.
Jan.	5	To Cash......	14	175	10	Jan.	1	By Cash......	13	100	00
,,	10	,, do.	,,	77	50	,,	8	,, do.	14	125	00
						,,	12	,, do.	,,	27	60
				252	60					252	60

The three Personal Accounts in this set, viz., Reid, Thompson and Robertson's, exhibit the various conditions which Personal Accounts can assume at the time of being closed. Reid owes me ; I owe Thompson ; Robertson and I owe each other nothing. A Ledger, containing ten thousand Personal Accounts, could not show to the pupil any new phase of this kind of account—except some indebted person were to fail, then his account would be closed by the Profit and Loss Account.

W. R. ORR.

DR. BALANCE. CR.

1868.			L.F.	$	C.	1868.			L.F.	$	C.
Jan.	14	To Cash......	1	246	55	Jan.	14	By J. Thompson	2	182	05
,,		,, Wm. Reid.	,,	185	50	,,	,,	,, Stock	1	250	00
				432	05					432	05

* This account is not included in the Trial Balance (See Day Book, page 17), because both sides are alike and consequently cannot affect it. It facilitates the work of making out a Trial Balance if all the accounts which close themselves are left out.

W. R. ORR.

BOOK-KEEPING.

THIRD SET.

CASH AND ANOTHER REAL ACCOUNT.

Accounts of any kind of property, as Cash, Goods of any kind, Ships, Houses, Shares in Companies, etc., are called *real* accounts, *i. e.*, accounts of things which belong to me.

One object of Book-keeping is to keep a record of my property, how it is vested, whether in money, or goods, or lands; and as, in the course of mercantile transactions, it is continually varying, it is necessary to keep an exact account of these variations. Another object is to ascertain whether I be losing or gaining by my transactions, and how much I may have gained or lost during any given time; and also, by what particular transactions the gains were made, or the losses sustained. Now these objects are effected by keeping the real accounts, which are, as has been explained, accounts of my property of whatever kind it may be.

The following transactions are intended to show how a person's Stock may pass from one kind of property to another, how an account is kept of it, and how it is ascertained that profit has been made, or loss sustained. Then suppose that I deal in but one article, viz., Wine, and that by the pipe; and that I buy and sell for Cash : so that my Stock is always either in Cash or in pipes of Wine. For by always purchasing and selling for Cash, I owe nobody anything; nor does any one owe me anything; so that I require to keep no accounts with any other person. I have, therefore, no Personal Accounts.

THIRD SET.
WASTE BOOK.

TORONTO, 1st JANUARY, 1868.

J.F.		$	C.
1	I have on hand, Cash ....$ 2000 00 Wine, 50 pipes, at $350 per pipe 17500 00	19500	00
	_____February 1st._____		
1	Sold to Williamson & Co., for Cash,— 6 pipes of Wine, at $375................	2250	00
	_____10_____		
1	Sold to James Allen & Co., for Cash,— 10 pipes of Wine, at $377................	3770	00
	_____March 12th._____		
1	Bought of William Adams, for Cash,— 17 pipes, at $366......................	6222	00
	_____30_____		
1	Sold to Michael Sullivan & Co., for Cash,— 50 pipes at $375.....................	18750	00
	_____April 2nd._____		
1	Bought, for Cash, from Joseph Staunton,— 37 pipes. at $375.....................	13875	00
	_____15_____		
1	Sold, for Cash, to James Allen & Co., 3 pipes, at $406......................	1218	00
	_____May 5th._____		
1	Sold, for Cash, to Chas. Thompson,— 1 pipe, at $410......................	410	00
	_____26_____		
1	Sold to Anderson & Co., for Cash,— 5 pipes, which had sustained injury, at $320	1600	00

THIRD SET.

TORONTO, JUNE 16TH, 1868.

J.F.		$	C.
2	Bought of Wm. Adams, for Cash,—		
	18 pipes, at $325 ....$5850 00		
	5 do., at $355 .... 1775 00		
		7625	00
	_____ 18 _____		
2	Sold to Thomas Brett, for Cash,—		
	2 pipes, at $365	730	00
	_____ 30 _____		
2	Sold to M. Sullivan & Co., for Cash,—		
	10 pipes, at $345 ....$3450 00		
	7 do., at $375 .... 2625 00		
		6075	00
	_____ July 1st. _____		
2	Took Stock, and found on hand,—		
	Cash.............................$9081 00		
	Wine, 20 pipes, at $350......... 7000 00		
	Do., 13 do., at $365........... 4745 00		
		20826	00

To arrange these transactions in a Ledger, so as to effect the purposes of Book-keeping with regard to them, three accounts must be opened—one for Stock, a second for Cash, and a third for Wine. On the Cr. side of the Stock Account is stated the amount of Cash, and the value of the Wine on hand; and the account remains in that state till the accounts are to be balanced; that is to say, till I wish to know whether I have gained or lost by the transactions, and to what amount either of loss or gain. All the transactions, therefore, are entered in the other two accounts. And here the general rule is to be observed, that whatever kind of property comes in, is to be entered on the Dr. side of its own account; and whatever kind goes out, is to be entered on the Cr. side of its own account;

THIRD SET.

from this it will follow that whatever is entered on the Dr. side of one account will be entered on the Cr. side of the other, and *vice versa;* because, as often as Cash comes in, Wine goes out, and as often as Wine comes in, Cash goes out.

To assist the pupil in posting his Ledger, let him previously write an exercise upon these transactions upon a loose slip of paper, the object of which would be to distinguish, in each transaction, which of the accounts is Dr., and which Cr. This will prepare him for understanding the nature and uses of a Journal, a book of which nothing has yet been said. The exercise is to be in the following form, omitting, of course, the directions printed in small type :

TORONTO, 1st JANUARY, 1868.

		$	c.
Sundries Dr. to Stock,—			
Cash ....$ 2000 00			
Wine, 50 pipes 17500 00			
		19500	00
1st February.			
Cash Dr. to Wine,—			
Sold to Williamson & Co.,			
6 pipes, at $375		2250	00
The Cash came in, and Wine went out, therefore Cash is Dr.			

THIRD SET.

TORONTO, 10th FEBRUARY, 1868.

	$	c.

Cash Dr. to Wine,—
    Sold to James Allen & Co.,
       10 pipes, at $377 ....
	3770	00

Here also Cash came in, and Wine went out, so that Cash is Dr.		

12th March.

	$	c.

Wine Dr. to Cash,—
    Bought of William Adams,
       17 pipes, at $366 ....
	6222	00

Here the Wine came in, and Cash went out, therefore Wine is Dr.		

The last of the entries in the Waste Book, namely, the taking of Stock, and finding how much Cash and Wine remain on hand, is to be written in the exercise, thus:

	$	c.

Balance Dr.,—
    To Cash .... $ 9081 00
    " Wine 11745 00
	20826	00

Third Set—Directions.

Having finished all the entries in this form on a loose slip of paper, let the pupil copy them in the same form and order, into a book ruled like the Waste Book, and which is called the Journal, (with double columns to the right).

Having written the Journal, he then opens his three accounts in the Ledger; one for Stock, a second for Cash, and a third for Wine. Instead of posting the Ledger from the Waste Book, as in the former Sets, let him now post from the Journal.

In the first entry, Sundries are Dr. to Stock. The word Sundries always means in Book-keeping, not sundry or several articles, but sundry or several accounts. Here it stands for the two accounts mentioned immediately afterwards, Cash and Wine. These accounts are Drs. Let him therefore turn to the Cash Account, and enter the Cash on hand on the Dr. side, writing before it, " To Stock." Also to the Wine Account, and on the Dr. side write, " To Stock," prefixing the date, and adding the number of pipes in the proper column, and the amount in the money column. Let him then turn to the Stock Account, Cr. side, and after writing the date as before, write, " By Sundries," adding the whole sum, $19500.00.

Let him then proceed to the other entries in the Journal, and wherever he finds one account made Dr. to another, let him turn to the Dr. side of that account, which is made Dr., and write, "To——," mentioning the other account; and then let him turn to the Cr. side of that other account, and write, " By——," mentioning the first account. Thus, when he finds such an entry as " Cash Dr. to Wine, $2250.00," he turns to the Dr. side of the Cash Account, and after the date writes, " To Wine, $2250.00 ;" he then turns to the Wine Account, and on the Cr. side he writes, after the date, " By Cash, $2250 00," also inserting in an inner column the quantity of Wine mentioned in the entry.

Third Set—Directions.

The Wine Account will appear as in the note below,* and the Cash Account as in the former Set.

*Dr.,   WINE.   CONTRA.,   Cr.

1868.			pipes	$	c.	1868.			pipes	$	c.
Jan.	1	To Stock	50	17500	00	Jan.	1	By Cash	6	2250	00
,,	,,	,, Cash	17	6222	00	,,	10	,, Do.	10	3770	00
Mch.	30	,, Profit and Loss† ..		1398	00	Mch.	30	,, Do.	50	18750	00
						,,	,,	,, Balance..	1	350	00
			67	25120	00				67	25120	00

† The words "Profit and Loss" are the title of an account, which will be explained after.

Third Set—Directions.

Having posted all the entries but the last, which states the amount of Stock on hand, let the pupil make his Trial Balance as in the former Set.

This being found correct, he must proceed to balance the accounts. He first balances the Cash Account, as in Sets one (1) and two (2). The Wine Account is differently balanced. The balance of that account consists in the quantity of Wine remaining on hand.

This he will find by balancing the inner columns, in which the quantity bought and sold is stated.* Add up the number of pipes on each side, and on a slate or separate bit of paper, subtract the one sum from the other ; and if there be a difference, enter it at the bottom of the side on which is the smallest quantity, which must be the Cr. side; for no more could be sent out than came in—and write before it, "By Balance on hand."

A value must then be affixed to the quantity on hand, which, in real business, is the true value of the article in question, without the addition of any profit. Compute, then, the value of the whole Wine on hand, and enter the sum in the money column.

Add up, then, the money columns on the Dr. and Cr. side, on a slate or loose slip of paper, subtract the least from the greatest, and enter the difference on the side that is least. This difference, however, is not the balance of the account, *i. e.*, it is neither what property I have in it, nor what I owe upon it, but it is the sum that I have lost or gained by the transactions recorded. On the Dr. side has been entered the value of all that I had when I began, and of all that came in afterwards ; on the Cr. side has been entered the value of all that went out, and of all that remains on hand. The difference, therefore, must be my loss or gain.

---

* These columns answer the purpose of a Stock Ledger, or Warehouse book, which is or ought to be kept by every wholesale house.

W. R. ORR.

I enter the difference then on the smallest side, prefixing not "To or By *Balance*," but "To or By *Profit and Loss.*"

If the Dr. side was the smaller side, I enter upon it, "To Profit and Loss;" if the Cr. side, upon it, "By Profit and Loss."

This entry requires the opening of a new account, namely, Profit and Loss, the use of which is to keep an account of my gains or losses; and having entered on the Dr. side of the Wine Account, "To Profit and Loss for my net gain," I turn to the Cr. side of the Profit and Loss Account, and enter, "By Wine for my net gain," entering the amount in the money column.

Add up now the two sides of the Wine Account, which will be found equal, and which closes that account.

In order to close the Set, open an account for Balance, and enter upon it the balances of the Cash and Wine Accounts. As the Balances are entered on the Cr. sides of these accounts, they must be entered on the Dr. side of the Balance Account, "To Cash" and "To Wine."

Then close the Profit and Loss Accounts. This is done, as in the other cases, by adding up both sides separately, and subtracting the one from the other. But, in this Set, nothing is entered on the Dr. side; we must, therefore, enter the whole of what is on the Cr. side, on the Dr. side. As this is gain, or an addition to my original Stock, I enter it, "To Stock for my net gain." I then turn to the Stock Account, and on the Cr. side I write, By Profit and Loss, entering the same sum.

Proceed now to close the Balance Account, by adding up both sides of it, subtracting the one from the other, and entering the difference upon the smallest side. This difference would be all that I possess, after deducting from it all that I owe, and, therefore, is called my net estate.

Third Set—Directions.

In this Set I have no debts due to me or by me; nothing, therefore, is on the Cr. side of this account; but, I add up the Dr. side, and enter the whole on the Cr. side, writing, "By Stock for my net estate;" I then turn to the Stock Account, and on the Dr. side enter, "To Balance for my net estate;" and if the two sides of the Stock Account be now equal, the books have been kept correctly; not otherwise. The reason of this is, that the Dr. side of the Stock Account now contains all that I possess, after deducting from it whatever I owe, and also whatever I may have lost. The Cr. side contains all that I had when I commenced, with the addition of whatever I gained since. These statements, therefore, are both of them statements of my actual property, and, if correct, must be alike.

Third Set—Questions.

QUESTIONS ON THE THIRD SET.

What are *Real* Accounts? What two objects are effected by keeping Real Accounts? What are the transactions in this Set intended to show? Why is it not necessary to keep Personal Accounts in the following transactions? After the Waste Book has been copied out, how many accounts must be opened in the Ledger, and for what? What general rule is to be observed? What book do you post from into the Ledger? How would you enter the number of pipes of Wine? In posting from the Journal, what would you do when you find one account made Dr. to another? What is the Trial Balance? What is to be done when the Trial Balance is found to be correct? What value do you give to Stock on hand? On which side do you enter Profit and Loss? How would you close the Set? What is your net estate?

THIRD SET.

CASH

AND

ANOTHER REAL ACCOUNT

JOURNAL.*

FOL. 1

TORONTO, 1st JANUARY, 1868.

L.F		P.D.B	$	C.	$	C.
1	Sundries Dr. to Stock,—	23				
1	Cash		2000	00		
2	Wine, 50 pipes, at $350.........		17500	00		
					19500	00

——————— 1st February. ———————

| 1 | Cash Dr. to Wine,— | 23 | | | | |
| 2 | Sold 6 pipes, at $375 .... | | | | 2250 | 00 |

The Cash came in, and Wine went out, therefore Cash is Dr.

——————— 10 ———————

| 1 | Cash Dr. to Wine,— | 23 | | | | |
| 2 | Sold 10 pipes, at $377 .... | | | | 3770 | 00 |

——————— 12th March. ———————

| 2 | Wine Dr. to Cash,— | 23 | | | | |
| 1 | Bought 17 pipes, at $366 .... | | | | 6222 | 00 |

Here the Wine came in, and Cash went out, therefore Wine is Dr.

——————— 30th. ———————

| 1 | Cash Dr. to Wine,— | 23 | | | | |
| 2 | Sold 50 pipes, at $375 .... | | | | 18750 | 00 |

——————— 2nd April. ———————

| 2 | Wine Dr. to Cash,— | 23 | | | | |
| 1 | Bought 37 pipes, at $375 .... | | | | 13875 | 00 |

——————— 15 ———————

| 1 | Cash Dr. to Wine,— | 23 | | | | |
| 2 | Sold 3 pipes, at $406 .... | | | | 1218 | 00 |

——————— 5th May. ———————

| 1 | Cash Dr. to Wine,— | 23 | | | | |
| 2 | Sold 1 pipe, at $410 .... | | | | 410 | 00 |

——————— 26 ———————

| 1 | Cash Dr. to Wine—, | 23 | | | | |
| 2 | Sold 5 pipes, at $320 .... | | | | 1600 | 00 |

* The Journal, in real business, is now, very properly, falling into disuse.—W. R. ORR.
† L. F. (Ledger Folio). P. D. B. (Page Day Book.)

Third Set—Journal.

FOL. 2

TORONTO, 16TH JUNE, 1868.

L.F.		P.D.B	$	C.	$	G.
2	Wine Dr. to Cash,—	24				
1	Bought 18 pipes, at $325		5850	00		
	Do. 5 do., ,, 355		1775	00		
					7625	00
	———— 18th. ————					
1	Cash Dr. to Wine,—	24				
2	Sold 2 pipes, at $365				730	00
	———— 30th. ————					
1	Cash Dr. to Wine,—	24				
2	Sold 10 pipes, at $345		3450	00		
	Do. 7 do., ,, 376		2632	00		
					6082	00
	———— 1st July. ————					
2	Balance Dr. to Sundries,—	24				
1	Cash		9081	00		
2	*Wine, 33 pipes		11745	00		
					20826	00

* In taking Stock of the Merchandize on hand, at the time of closing the Books, the actual number of pieces, or the weight, or measure of all the articles must be accurately ascertained, and calculated at what it cost when laid down in the warehouse. It is only from this data that the Profit or Loss can be fairly calculated.

W. B. ORR.

Third Set—Ledger.

STOCK.

Dr.									Cr.	
1868.			L.F	$	c.	1868.			*J F	$	c.
June	30	To Balance ..	2	20826	00	Jan.	1	By Sundries ..	1	19500	00
						June	30	,, Profit & Loss	L..F 2	1326	00
				20826	00					20826	00
						July	1	By Balance ..		20826	00

CASH.

Dr.									Cr.		
1868.			J.F	$	c.	1868.			J.F	$	c.
Jan.	1	To Stock	1	2000	00	Mar.	12	By Wine	1	6222	00
Feb.	1	,, Wine	,,	2250	00	April	2	,, do.......	,,	13875	00
,,	10	,, do.......	,,	3770	00	June	16	,, do.......	2	7625	00
Mar.	30	,, do.......	,,	18750	00				L.F		
April	15	,, do.......	,,	1218	00	June	30	,, Balance....	2	9081	00
May	5	,, do.......	,,	410	00						
,,	26	,, do.......	,,	1600	00						
June	18	,, do.......	2	730	00						
,,	30	,, do.......	,,	6075	00						
				36803	00					36803	00
July	1	To Balance ..		9081	00						

Third Set—Ledger.

FOL. 2

DR.   WINE.   **CR.**

FOL. 2

1868.			Ps.	J. F.	$	c.	1868.			Ps.	J. F.	$	c.
Jan.	1	To Stock	50	1	17500	00	Feb.	1	By Cash	6	1	2250	00
Mar.	12	,, Cash	17	,,	6222	00	,,	10	,, do.	10	,,	3770	00
Apr'l	2	,, do.	37	,,	13875	00	Mar.	30	,, do.	50	,,	18750	00
June	16	,, do.	23	2	7625	00	Apr'l	15	,, do.	3	,,	1218	00
				L. F.			May	5	,, do.	1	,,	410	00
June	30	,, Profit & Loss		2	1326	00	,,	26	,, do.	5	,,	1600	00
							June	18	,, do.	2	2	730	00
							,,	30	,, do.	17	,,	6075	00
							June	30	,, Balance	33	,,	11745	00
					127					46548	00		
										127		46548	00
July	1	To Balance	33		11745	00							

DR.   PROFIT AND LOSS.   **CR.**

1868.			L. F.	$	c.	1868.			L. F.	$	c.
June	30	To Stock	1	1326	00	June	30	By Wine	2	1326	00

DR.   BALANCE.   **CR.**

1868.			L.F	$	c.	1868.			L.F	$	c.
June	30	To Cash	1	9081	00	June	30	By Stock	1	20826	00
,,	,,	,, Wine	2	11745	00						
				20826	00					20826	00

BOOK-KEEPING.

FOURTH SET.

CASH ACCOUNT, WITH A GENERAL GOODS ACCOUNT.

In those trades in which goods are sold in small quantities, it is impossible to keep an account of every article sold, so as to be able to balance the different kinds of goods, by the quantity received and given out, as appearing on an inner column of the account of them. The description of goods also, in which trades are conducted, may be so numerous, that to attempt to trace every article by entries in the books, would require an expense in clerkship far beyond what the profits would afford; and create a complexity of books which would rather bewilder the accounts than fulfil the proper objects of Book-keeping.

In such cases it is usual to keep a general account of goods, or to divide them under different heads, and to enter only the *value* of goods received and given out, disregarding the *kinds* and *quantities*.

The only variation that this occasions, is that the balance of the goods on hand must be obtained by actual examination of the quantity of every kind in the shop or warehouse, and by an estimation of the value of every article. This operation is called *taking Stock*, and must be performed as often as the trader wishes to know the state of his affairs.

In the following transactions nothing is bought or sold on credit, but are all Cash transactions. The accounts, therefore, that are necessary, are merely a Cash Account and a Goods Account, with those fictitious Accounts, such as Stock, Profit and Loss, and Balance, which are necessary for balancing and closing the books.

FOURTH SET.

Write out the transactions in Set 4 of the Waste Book, as directed in the former Sets.

Proceed then to journalize them in the Journal. The first entry in the Day Book, which states what you have on hand, enter in the Journal, thus :—

		$	c.
Sundries Dr. to Stock,—			
Cash ....$	1598 00		
Goods	10088 50		
		11686	50

Or, more simply,—

		$	c.
Stock Cr.,—			
By Cash....................$	1598 00		
„ Goods	10088 50		
		11686	50

Then proceed to the other entries in their order, taking care to make what comes in always Dr. to what goes out, in the following form :—

	$	c.
Dr. Goods,—		
To Cash paid Waddell & Co	538	80

	$	c.
Dr. Goods,—		
To Cash paid Thos. White, for printing 500 copies Murray's Grammar	225	50

	$	c.
Dr. Cash,—		
To Goods, amount of this day's sales	136	25

BOOK-KEEPING.
WASTE BOOK.
TORONTO, 1st JANUARY, 1868.

J.F.		$	C.
1	Inventory of my Effects,— I have in ready money........$ 1598 00 Goods 10088 50	11686	50
	1		
1	Paid Waddell & Co., for Goods	538	80
	Here Goods are Dr. to Cash, because Goods came in, and Cash went out.		
	1		
1	Paid Thomas White, for printing 500 copies Murray's Grammar	225	50
	1		
1	Sales this day	136	25
	Here Cash came in, and Goods went out, therefore Cash is Dr. to Goods.		
	2		
1	Paid John Cummings, for Books, per invoice..	78	60
	2		
1	Paid William Wilson, for Binding	68	80
	2		
1	Sales this day	658	45
	4		
1	Received for 50 copies Murray's Grammar, at 60 c.	30	00
	4		
1	Paid Curry & Co., their account for Books ..	95	60

FOURTH SET. 41

TORONTO, 4TH JANUARY, 1868.

J.F.		$	c.
2	Bought from McDonnell & Co., Printing Paper, per invoice, and paid Cash	138	45
	——————— 4 ———————		
2	Sold 25 copies Murray's Grammar, for Cash, at 60c.	15	00
	——————— 4 ———————		
2	Sales this day	88	20
	——————— 5 ———————		
2	Remitted Wesley & Co., on account of Books.	225	60
	——————— 5 ———————		
2	Received from Wm. McCombe, Belfast, for Goods sold him	435	00
	——————— 5 ———————		
2	Sales this day	318	80
	——————— 6 ———————		
2	Took Stock, and found,— Cash on hand ....$1908 35 Goods do. 9987 75	11896	10

DIRECTIONS.

Having thus gone over all the entries in the Day Book, and posted them in the Journal, take your Ledger, and open three accounts—one of Stock, a second of Cash, and a third of Goods, as formerly.

Proceed now to post into the Ledger from the Journal, according to the directions given in Set 3.

Book-keeping.

Having finished this operation, you are prepared to balance the books; that is, to ascertain whether you have gained or lost by the transactions. Before balancing each account, make a Trial Balance, as directed in Set 3.

Having found this correct, turn now to the Cash Account, and balance it as in all the former Sets.

The Goods Account is balanced differently. You must first insert on the Cr. side of that account the value of the goods on hand. In real business this, as has been said, is ascertained by what is called taking Stock, in which operation the person in business examines all the goods that he has on hand, and enters them, valued at the price which they cost him, or rather the price that they would bring in the wholesale market. The goods on hand constituted the balance of the Goods Account, and are entered at the bottom of that account, on the Cr. side, " By Balance for Goods on hand."

Add up now, as in the Wine Account of the Third Set, the two sides, and the Cr. side being greater, put the difference on the other side, writing before it, "To Profit and Loss." Then open an account for Profit and Loss, and on the Cr. side write, " By Goods," adding the same sum in the money column.

We are now prepared to close the books. For this purpose, open, as in Set 3, an account for Balance, and enter in it the Balance of the Cash and Goods Account. The Balance of these accounts appearing on the Cr. side, you put them on the Dr. side of the Balance Account, writing, " To Cash " and " To Goods," adding the sums in which these accounts are credited by Balance.

The first account to be closed is the Profit and Loss, as in Set 3.

Fourth Set—Directions.

You next close the Balance Account, as also directed in Set 3, carrying the difference of the two sides to the Stock Account, as there directed.

And if the Dr. and Cr. side of the Stock Account be thus made equal, the books have been correctly kept.

QUESTIONS ON THE FOURTH SET.

When goods are sold in small quantities, would you keep a separate account for each article sold? How would you manage? How, then, would you find the balance of goods on hand? What is this operation called? How often must it be performed? Since, in the following transactions, there is nothing bought or sold on credit, what are the only accounts necessary? What are you to do after having written the Waste Book? When you have posted the Journal, what next? What accounts would you open in your Ledger? How would you balance the Goods Account? At what price would you value the goods on hand? When, upon adding up, you find a difference in the two sides, what do you do with that difference? In what other account do you enter this? How do you close the books? How do you know when they have been correctly kept?

FOURTH SET.

CASH ACCOUNT
WITH
A GENERAL GOODS ACCOUNT.

Fourth Set—Journal.

FOL. 1

TORONTO, 1st JANUARY, 1868.

L.F.		P.D.B	$	C.	$	C.
1	Sundries Dr. to Stock,—	40				
1	Cash		1598	00		
2	Goods		10088	50		
					11686	50

——————— 1 ———————

2	Dr. Goods,—	40				
1	To Cash paid Waddell & Co......				538	80

——————— 1 ———————

2	Dr. Goods,—	40				
1	To Cash paid Thos. White				225	50

——————— 1 ———————

1	Dr. Cash,—	40				
2	To Goods, amount of sales this day				136	25

——————— 2 ———————

2	Dr. Goods,—	40				
1	To Cash paid John Cumming				78	60

——————— 2 ———————

2	Dr. Goods,—	40				
1	To Cash paid Wm. Wilson				68	80

——————— 2 ———————

1	Dr. Cash,—	40				
2	To Goods, amount of this day's sales				658	45

——————— 4 ———————

1	Dr. Cash,—	40				
2	To Goods, 50 copies Murray's Grammar				30	00

——————— 4 ———————

2	Dr. Goods,—	40				
1	To Cash paid Curry & Co				95	60

Fourth Set—Journal.

FOL. 2

TORONTO, 4TH JANUARY, 1868.

L.F.		P.D.B	$	C.	$	C.
2	Dr. Goods,—	41				
1	To Cash paid McDonnell & Co. ..				138	45
	———— 4 ————					
1	Dr. Cash,—	41				
2	To Goods, 25 copies Murray's Grammar				15	00
	———— 4 ————					
1	Dr. Cash,—	41				
2	To Goods, amount of this day's sales				88	20
	———— 5 ————					
2	Dr. Goods,—	41				
1	To Cash remitted Wesley & Co. ..				225	60
	———— 5 ————					
1	Dr. Cash,—	41				
2	To Goods received from Wm. McCombe				435	00
	———— 5 ————					
1	Dr. Cash,—	41				
2	To Goods, amount of this day's sales				318	80
	———— 6 ————					
2	Dr. Balance,—	41				
1	To Cash		1908	35		
2	,, Goods....................		9987	75		
					11896	10

Fourth Set—Ledger.

FOL. 1

Dr.   STOCK   Cr.

1868.			L.F	$	C.	1868.			J.F	$	C.
Jan.	6	To Balance ..	2	11896	10	Jan.	1	By Sundries ..	1	11686	50
						,,	6	,, Profit & Loss	2	209	60
				11896	10					11896	10
						,,	7	,, Balance....		11896	10

Dr.   CASH   Cr.

1868.			J.F	$	C.	1868.			J.F	$	C.
Jan.	1	To Stock	1	1598	00	Jan.	1	By Goods	1	538	80
,,	,,	,, Goods	,,	136	25	,,	,,	,, do	1	225	50
,,	2	,, do	,,	658	45	,,	2	,, do	,,	78	60
,,	4	,, do	,,	30	00	,,	,,	,, do	,,	68	80
,,	,,	,, do	2	15	00	,,	4	,, do	,,	95	60
,,	,,	,, do	,,	88	20	,,	,,	,, do	2	138	45
,,	5	,, do	,,	435	00	,,	5	,, do	,,	225	60
,,	,,	,, do	,,	318	80				L.F		
						,,	6	,, Balance ..	2	1908	35
				3279	70					3279	70
,,	7	To Balance ..		1908	35						

Fourth Set—Ledger.

FOL. 2

Dr.   GOODS.   Cr. FOL. 2

1868.			J.F	$	C.	1868.			J.F	$	C.
Jan.	1	To Stock	1	10088	50	Jan.	1	By Cash	1	136	25
,,	,,	,, Cash......	,,	538	80	,,	2	,, do	,,	658	45
,,	,,	,, do	,,	225	50	,,	4	,, do	,,	30	00
,,	2	,, do	,,	78	60	,,	,,	,, do	2	15	00
,,	,,	,, do	,,	68	80	,,	,,	,, do	,,	88	20
,,	4	,, do	,,	95	60	,,	5	,, do	,,	435	00
,,	,,	,, do	2	138	45	,,	,,	,, do	,,	318	80
,,	5	,, do	,,	225	60				L.F		
			L.F			,,	6	,, Balance ..	2	9987	75
,,	6	,, Profit & Loss	2	209	60						
				11669	45					11669	45
,,	7	To Balance ..		9987	75						

Dr.   PROFIT AND LOSS.   Cr.

1868.			L.F	$	C.	1868.			L.F	$	
Jan.	6	To Stock	1	209	60	Jan	6	By Goods	2	209	60

Dr.   BALANCE.   Cr.

1868.			L.F	$	C.	1868.			L.F	$	C.
Jan.	6	To Cash......	1	1908	35	Jan.	6	By Stock	1	11896	10
,,	,,	,, Goods	2	9987	75						
				11896	10					11896	10

BOOK-KEEPING

FIFTH SET.

EXAMPLES OF PERSONAL ACCOUNTS

IN

ADDITION TO REAL ACCOUNTS.

When goods are bought or sold on credit, it becomes necessary, as was explained under Set 2, to keep an account of our dealings with every person with whom we transact business on credit, that we may know what they owe to us, or what we owe to them. The accounts which we keep with other persons are called Personal Accounts, and the rule for keeping them is, that every transaction in which they receive anything from us, or that brings them into our debt, or that takes us out of their debt, is placed on the Dr. side of their account; and that every transaction in which we receive anything from them, or that brings us into their debt, or relieves them from being in our debt, is placed on the Cr. side of their account.

We have, therefore, found three kinds of accounts used in Book-keeping, namely,—1st. My own accounts, called also Real Accounts, which contain accounts of my property divided into as many particulars as I find necessary. These are not headed with my name, but with the names of the property, an account of which is to be kept;—as Cash, Goods, any particular kind of Goods, Houses, Ships, etc., in all of which accounts the kind of property with which the accounts is headed signifies myself, in regard to such property. 2nd. Accounts of other persons with me, called sometimes Personal Accounts, described above; and 3rd. Accounts of gains or losses, such as Profit and Loss, Discount, Rent, Charges, etc., all receipts or expenses, for which no direct return is given or received.

Book-keeping.

To these is to be added, the Stock and Balance Accounts. These are used merely to show at one view the state of my affairs, at some particular time. The Stock Account, commences with a statement of what I possess on entering into business, and after every balance of my books. The Balance Account shows, on examining the state of my affairs, on the one side, all that I possess, and all that is due to me; on the other side, all that is due by me to others.

These two accounts, therefore, are used merely in commencing or closing a set of books, no entry being made in them between one balance and another.

The chief of the accounts called fictitious, more properly accounts of gain or loss, is the Profit and Loss Account itself, the others being only subdivisions of it, and being concentrated into it, in balancing the books.

DIRECTIONS

Proceed, as in the former cases, to copy the following transactions in the Day Book.

In posting the Journal, remember that the transactions are upon credit, except when the contrary is specified; as when it is said, Bought *for Cash*, or Sold *for Cash;* in these cases you journalize as in Set 3, making Cash Dr. when it comes in, and Cr. when it goes out. But when sales are made to persons mentioned, and it is not said that they paid cash, make that person Dr. to the goods sold to him; and when you purchase goods of any person, and it is not mentioned that you paid cash for them, make yourself, that is, your account of goods, Dr. to that person. When cash is received, **while no property is given for it**, as gifts or legacies, make Cash Dr. to Profit and Loss. The Cash came in, therefore it is Dr.; and as it is clear gain, it is made Dr. to Profit and Loss Account, which

Fifth Set—Directions.

contains the accounts of gains and losses. When Cash goes out, without any return of property that can be added to Stock, as in paying wages, rent, losing money, etc., then Cash is Cr. by Profit and Loss. The Cash went out, therefore it is Cr.; and as nothing was received for it, Profit and Loss is its Dr. In manufacturing establishments, the wages of workmen are paid for the addition made to the value of the raw material manufactured, and, therefore, ought to be put to the *debit* of the goods on which they are expended.

Having finished the Journal, open accounts as before, for Stock, for Cash, and for Goods, and also for every person who is made Dr. or Cr. in the Journal. You then go over every entry in the Journal in order, as in the former sets, posting them into their proper accounts in the Ledger, every item being posted on the Dr. side of one account, and on the Cr. side of another.

Having made a Trial Balance, as in the former sets, proceed to dalance the Cash and Goods Accounts as before, the balance of the Goods Account being the quantity of goods on hand, taken by inventory. Then balance each of the Personal Accounts, adding up the two sides of each, and putting the difference, as before, on the smallest side, saying, "To Balance," if it be added to the Dr. side, and "By Balance," if to the Cr. side.

Add up the two sides of the Goods Account, after the balance of goods on hand has been added to the Cr. side, and put the difference to the smallest side, saying, "To Profit and Loss," if it be added to the Dr. side, and "By Profit and Loss," if it be added to tne Cr. side.

Open then a Balance Account, and enter all the balances of the different accounts as before. If the balance of any account stands on the Dr. side, enter it on the Cr. side of the Balance Account, saying, "By ———," (the account from which it is taken), and *vice versa*.

Fifth Set—Directions.

Balance the Profit and Loss Account, placing the difference of the two sides to the Dr. or Cr. of Stock, and post it in the Stock Account.

Then balance the Balance Account, placing the difference of that account also to Stock; and if the two sides of the Stock Account are equal, when the balance of these two accounts is posted, the books are correct.

BOOK-KEEPING.

ON TRACING TRANSACTIONS

FROM

ONE BOOK TO ANOTHER.

It is often necessary to find how a transaction recorded in the Waste book, has been entered in the Journal, or how it has been posted in the Ledger; or, on the contrary, to trace back some entry in the Ledger, to the original record of it in the Waste Book.

This is effected by the number of the page, or folio of the book into which any entry is made, being entered upon the book from which it is taken; and also the number of the page of the book from which an entry is posted, being entered in the book into which it is posted. It is not necessary thus to connect the Waste Book and Journal, because the order of the dates being followed in both books, the date will be sufficient guide from one to the other.* But as this order is not followed in the Ledger, it is necessary to connect the entries in the Journal. When, then, an entry is made from the Journal to the Ledger, as above described, it is usual to note on the margin of the Journal, the two or more folios into which the transaction has been posted, and to mark in a column, ruled in the Ledger for that purpose, the corresponding Ledger folio. Entries can be traced from the Ledger to the Journal by the date. Thus:

---

* It is better to enter the page or folio in all cases; it is a much readier reference than the date.

W. R. ORR.

Fifth Set—Directions.

		IN THE JOURNAL.	$	c.
		6		
2/17		Dr. Cash to Tobacco............................	100	00

The figures in the margin $\frac{2}{17}$ imply that the Cash Account is in folio 2 of the Ledger, and the Tobacco Account is in folio 17.

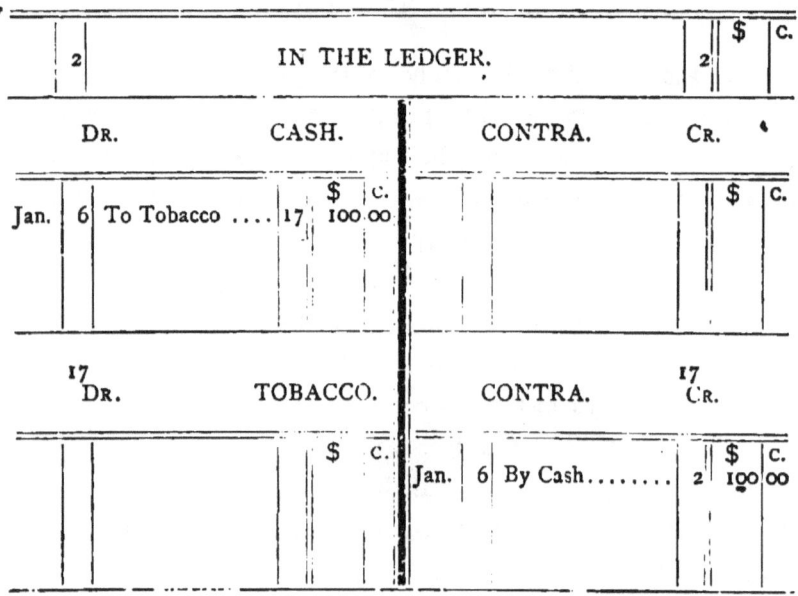

The number 17 in the column immediately beside the money column in the Cash Account, signifies that the Tobacco Account will be found at folio 17; and the number 2, in the corresponding column of the Tobacco Account, signifies that the Cash Account is in folio 2.*

---

* This mode of reference, from one account in the Ledger to another, is not in accordance with the general practice; it is the folio of the Journal that is entered opposite the money in the Ledger Account.

W. R. ORR.

BOOK-KEEPING.
WASTE BOOK.
TORONTO, 1st JANUARY, 1868.

J.F		$	c.
1	I have on hand,— Cash ....$1019 50 Goods 4868 45	5887	95
	_____1_____		
1	Received from John Black & Co.,— Goods, as per invoice	470	75
	_____1_____		
1	Received for Cash sales this day	52	87
	_____2_____		
1	Paid James White, on account	80	00
	_____2_____		
1	Received the late Mr. Gordon's Legacy, deducting duty	74	50
	This sum having been received without any return, it is Journalized —Cash Dr. to Profit and Loss.		
	_____2_____		
1	Received for Cash sales this day	54	85
	_____3_____		
1	Received from James White,— Edition of Euclid's Elements, per invoice	300	65
	_____3_____		
1	Received for Cash sales this day	45	48
	_____4_____		
1	Sold A. Macarthur,— 1 Euclid ....$ 1 50 1 Walker's Dictionary .... 2 10 6 Spelling Books, at 15 c..................... 90 50 Reading do., ,, 40 c................... 20 00	24	50

BOOK-KEEPING.

TORONTO, 4TH JANUARY, 1868.

J.F		$	c.
1	Paid James White, on account	160	00
	———————— 4 ————————		
1	Paid Clerk's Salary, one half year, ending this day	150	00
	Nothing being received for Clerk's salaries, that can be added to the amount of Stock, and the Cash going out, Profit and Loss is Dr. to Cash.		
	———————— 4 ————————		
2	Received for this day's shop sales	20	45
	———————— 5 ————————		
2	Remitted John Black & Co.,— On account	400	00
	———————— 5 ————————		
2	Received from James White,— Spelling Books, per invoice	11	20
	———————— 5 ————————		
2	Received for shop sales this day	61	50
	———————— 6 ————————		
2	Received from John Black & Co.,— Goods, per invoice	213	60
	———————— 6 ————————		
2	Sold A. Macarthur,— 24 Scripture Geography, at 10 c. ....$ 2 40 100 Maculloch's Reading, ,, 60 c. .... 60 00 20 Dictionaries, ,, 50 c. 10 00	72	40
	———————— 6 ————————		
2	Paid James White, on account	71	85
	———————— 6 ————————		
2	Paid half year's rent of Warehouse	200	00
	Rents are on the same footing with Salaries. and, therefore, Profit and Loss is Dr. to Cash for them.		

FIFTH SET.

TORONTO, 6TH JANUARY, 1868.

J.F		$	c.
2	Bought a house in Capel Street, and received for my bargain	80	00
	This $80 being clear gain, and the Cash being received, Cash is Dr. to Profit and Loss.		

——————————— 6 ———————————

| 2 | Received amount of this day's Cash sales .... | 31 | 64 |

——————————— 8 ———————————

| 2 | Received from A. Macarthur,— On account .... | 80 | 00 |

——————————— 8 ———————————

| 3 | Sold A. Macarthur,—
 10 Thompson's Arithmetic, at 60 c $6 00
 12   do.   Geography, ,, 40 c .... 4 80 | 10 | 80 |

——————————— 8 ———————————

| 3 | Remitted John Black & Co.,— On account .... | 240 | 00 |

——————————— 8 ———————————

| 3 | Received amount of this day's Cash sales .... | 48 | 87 |

——————————— 9 ———————————

| 3 | Lost a Bank Note, *value............................. | 40 | 00 |

——————————— 9 ———————————

| 3 | Took Stock, and found in my possession,—
 Cash .... $ 227 81
 Goods 5594 50
 Debts due to me .... 27 70 | 5850 | 01 |
| 3 | Debts due by me ....$44 35 | | |

* Nothing being received for this $40, and the Cash going out, Profit and Loss is Dr. to Cash.

Fifth Set—Questions.

QUESTIONS ON THE FIFTH SET.

What does the Fifth Set contain? What is the rule for keeping Personal Accounts? How many kinds of Accounts have we found used in Book-keeping? What is the first? The second? The third? What two accounts are used merely at the commencement and close of a set of books? What are Fictitious Accounts? What do you understand by *bought for Cash?* What, if the word Cash is omitted? How would you enter Cash when it comes in, without property going out? How would you enter Wages, Rent, Lost Money, etc.? How would you enter wages in a manufacturing establishment? What is to be done when the Journal is finished?

FIFTH SET.

PERSONAL ACCOUNTS
IN ADDITION TO
REAL ACCOUNTS.

JOURNAL.

FOL. 1

TORONTO, 1st JANUARY, 1868.

L. F.		P.D.B	$	C.	$	C.
1	Sundries Dr. to Stock,—	55				
1	Cash		1019	50		
2	Goods		4868	45		
					5887	95
	———— 1 ————					
2	Dr. Goods,—	55				
2	To John Black & Co.				470	75
	———— 1 ————					
1	Cash Dr.,—	55				
2	To Goods				52	87
	———— 2 ————					
2	Dr. James White,—	55				
1	To Cash				80	00
	———— 2 ————					
1	Dr. Cash,—	55				
3	To Profit and Loss				74	50
	———— 2 ————					
1	Dr. Cash,—	55				
2	To Goods				54	85
	———— 3 ————					
2	Dr. Goods,—	55				
2	To James White				300	65
	———— 3 ————					
1	Dr. Cash,—	55				
2	To Goods				45	48
	———— 4 ————					
3	Dr. A. Macarthur,—	55				
2	To Goods				24	50
	———— 4 ————					
2	Dr. James White,—	56				
1	To Cash				160	00
	———— 4 ————					
3	Dr. Profit and Loss,—	56				
1	To Cash				150	00

Fifth Set—Journal

TORONTO, 4TH JANUARY, 1868.

FOL. 2

L. F.		P.D.B	$	C.	$	C.
1	Dr. Cash,—	56				
2	To Goods				20	45
	——— 5 ———					
2	Dr. John Black & Co.,—	56				
1	To Cash				400	00
	——— 5 ———					
2	Dr. Goods,—	56				
2	To James White				11	20
	——— 5 ———					
1	Dr. Cash,—	56				
2	To Goods				61	50
	——— 6 ———					
2	Dr. Goods,—	56				
2	To John Black & Co............				213	60
	——— 6 ———					
3	Dr. A. Macarthur,—	56				
2	To Goods				72	40
	——— 6 ———					
2	Dr. James White,—	56				
1	To Cash				71	85
	——— 6 ———					
3	Dr. Profit and Loss,—	56				
1	To Cash				200	00
	——— 6 ———					
1	Dr. Cash,—	57				
3	To Profit and Loss				80	00
	——— 6 ———					
1	Dr. Cash,—	57				
2	To Goods				31	64
	——— 8 ———					
1	Dr. Cash,—	57				
3	To A. Macarthur...............				80	00

Fifth Set—Journal.

FOL. 3   TORONTO, 8TH JANUARY, 1868.

L. F.		P. D. B	$	C.	$	C.
3	Dr. A. Macarthur,—	57				
2	To Goods				10	80
	———— 8 ————					
2	Dr. John Black & Co.,—	57				
1	To Cash				240	00
	———— 8 ————					
1	Dr. Cash,—	57				
2	To Goods				48	87
	———— 9 ————					
3	Dr. Profit and Loss,—	57				
1	To Cash				40	00
	———— 9 ————					
3	Dr. Balance,—	57				
1	To Cash		227	81		
2	,, Goods		5594	50		
3	,, A. Macarthur.............		27	70	5850	01
3	Cr. Balance,—	57				
2	By John Black & Co.				44	35

LEDGER.

FOL. 1

Dr.   STOCK.   **Cr.**

1868.			L.F	$	c.	1868.			J.F	$	c.
Jan.	9	To Profit & Loss	3	82	29	Jan.	1	By Sundries ...	1	5887	95
,,	,,	,, Balance	,,	5805	66						
				5887	95					5887	95
						,,	10	,, Balance		5805	66

Dr.   CASH.   **Cr.**

1868.			J.F	$	c.	1868.			J.F	$	c.
Jan.	1	To Stock	1	1019	50	Jan.	2	By Jas. White.	1	80	00
,,	,,	,, Goods	,,	52	87	,,	4	,, Jas. White..	,,	160	00
,,	2	,, Profit & Loss	,,	74	50	,,	,,	,, Profit & Loss	,,	150	00
,,	,,	,, Goods	,,	54	85	,,	5	,, J. Black & Co	2	400	00
,,	3	,, do	,,	45	48	,,	6	,, Jas. White..	,,	71	85
,,	4	,, do	2	20	45	,,	,,	,, Profit & Loss	,,	200	00
,,	5	,, do	,,	61	50	,,	8	,, J. Black & Co	3	240	00
,,	6	,, Profit & Loss	,,	80	00	,,	9	,, Profit & Loss	,,	40	00
,,	,,	,, Goods	,,	31	64				L.F		
,,	8	,, A. Macarthur	,,	80	00	,,	,,	,, Balance ..	3	227	81
,,	,,	,, Goods	3	48	87						
				1569	66					1569	66
Jan.	10	To Balance ..		227	81						

Fifth Set—Ledger.

FOL. 2

DR.   GOODS.   CR.   FOL. 2

1868.			J.F	$	c.	1868.			J.F	$	c.
Jan.	1	To Stock	1	4868	45	Jan.	1	By Cash	1	52	87
,,	,,	,, J. Black & Co	,,	470	75	,,	2	,, do.	,,	54	85
,,	3	,, Jas. White..	,,	300	65	,,	3	,, do.	,,	45	48
,,	5	,, Jas. White..	2	11	20	,,	4	,, A. Macarthur	,,	24	50
,,	6	,, J. Black & Co	,,	213	60	,,	,,	,, Cash	2	20	45
			L.F			,,	5	,, do.	,,	61	50
,,	9	,, Profit & Loss	3	153	21	,,	6	,, A. Macarthur	,,	72	40
						,,	,,	,, Cash	,,	31	64
						,,	8	,, A. Macarthur	3	10	80
						,,	,,	,, Cash	,,	48	87
									L.F		
						,,	9	,, Balance	3	5594	50
				6017	86					6017	86
Jan.	10	To Balance		5594	50						

DR.   JOHN BLACK & Co.   CR.

1868.			J.F	$	c.	1868.			J.F	$	c.
Jan.	5	To Cash	2	400	00	Jan.	1	By Goods	1	470	75
,,	8	,, do.	3	240	00	,,	6	,, do.	2	213	60
			L.F								
,,	9	,, Balance	3	44	35						
				684	35					684	35
						Jan.	10	,, Balance		44	35

DR.   JAMES WHITE.   CR.

1868.			J.F	$	c.	1868.			J.F	$	c.
Jan.	2	To Cash	1	80	00	Jan.	3	By Goods	1	300	65
,,	4	,, do.	,,	160	00	,,	5	,, do.	2	11	20
,,	6	,, do.	2	71	85						
				311	85					311	85

Fifth Set—Ledger.

Dr.   PROFIT AND LOSS.   Cr.

Fol. 3 / Fol. 3

1868.			J.F	$	c.	1868.			J.F	$	c.
Jan.	4	To Cash......	1	150	00	Jan.	2	By Cash	1	74	50
,,	6	,, do	2	200	00	,,	6	,, do	2	80	00
,,	9	,, do	3	40	00	,,	9	,, Goods	,,	153	21
									L.F		
						,,	,,	,, Stock	1	82	29
				390	00					390	00

Dr.   A. MACARTHUR.   Cr.

1868.			J.F	$	c.	1868.			J.F	$	c.
Jan.	4	To Goods	1	24	50	Jan.	8	By Cash......	2	80	00
,,	6	,, do	2	72	40				L.F		
,,	8	,, do	3	10	80	,,	9	,, Balance ..	3	27	70
				107	70					107	70
Jan.	10	To Balance ..		27	70						

Dr.   BALANCE.   Cr.

1868.			L.F	$	c.	1868.			J.F	$	c.
Jan.	9	T Cash	1	227	81	Jan.	9	By J. Black & Co	2	44	35
,,	,,	,, Goods	2	5594	50				L.F		
,,	,,	,, A. Macarthur	3	27	70	,,	,,	,, Stock......	1	5805	66
				5850	10					5850	01

BOOK-KEEPING.

SIXTH SET.

EXAMPLES OF MY ACCOUNTS.

I. E.—Real Accounts, subdivided into various kinds of Goods; also of Transactions by Bills, with Discount, Interest, etc.

Copy the Day Book given below, as before.

In Journalizing, Credit Stock for all the articles in the inventory, and Debit it for all debits due either in Bills Payable or otherwise.

Every description of Goods that comes in is Dr.; and every description of Goods going out is made Cr. In both cases the quantity must be specified.

Bills Receivable are Bills for which I am to receive payment, or which are payable to me.

Bills Payable are Bills which I am to pay.

When I receive a Bill Receivable from any person, in payment of Goods bought by him, Bills Receivable are Dr. to Goods, because the Goods went out, and the Bill came in. When I give my own acceptance or note for Goods, then Goods are Dr. to Bills Payable; if the Bill was that of another person, previously entered to the *debit* of Bills Receivable, then Goods are Dr. to Bills Receivable.

If the Bill was received from a person with whom I have an account towards that account, then Bills Receivable is Dr. to that person; or if a Bill Receivable be paid to a person with whom I have credit, that person is Dr. to Bills Receivable. If I pay my own note, or give an acceptance to such a person, he is Dr. to Bills Payable.

SIXTH SET.

When a Bill is purchased for Cash to be remitted, it is usual not to enter the Bill in the Ledger account of Bills Receivable, but simply to make the person to whom it is remitted Dr. to Cash.

When one person's acceptance is paid to another person, with both of whom I have accounts, it is usual, instead of passing the Bill through the account of Bills Receivable, to make the person to whom the Bill was paid, Dr. to the acceptor of the Bill.

When I get Bills in my possession discounted, *i. e.*, when I receive Cash for them before they become due, the interest or discount being deducted, Bills Receivable are Cr. by the Cash received, and by the discount; because the Bills went out, and Cash came in for the amount of the Bills after deducting discount.

When I discount a Bill, *i. e.*, when I pay the Cash for it before it be due, receiving the interest or discount, Bills Receivable are Dr. to Cash and to Discount, both together making the amount of the Bill, because the Bill came in and the Cash went out.

When a person pays an account partly in Cash, partly in Bills, and discount is deducted from his account, he is Cr. by Cash, by Bills Receivable, and by Discount.

All charges, such as rent, wages, interest of money borrowed, may either be placed to the *debit* of the Profit and Loss Account, by posting them "Profit and Loss Dr. to Cash," or a separate account of them may be kept, and only the balance transferred to the Profit and Loss Account, when the books are to be balanced.

WASTE BOOK.

TORONTO, 1st JANUARY, 1868.

INVENTORY OF PROPERTY.

J.F.	Goods on hand.							$	c.	$	c.
		cwt.	qrs.	lbs.							
1	Alum	7	3	0	@ $2	80	℔ cwt..	21	70		
,,	Copperas......	23	0	0 ,,	1	15	,, do.	26	45		
,,	Tobacco	12	1	13 ,,	1	20	,, lb..	1485	60		
,,	Sugar	12	3	0 ,,	9	00	,, cwt..	114	75		
,,	Opium			73 ,,	2	45	,, lb..	178	85		
,,	Galls			146 ,,		50	,, do.	73	00		
,,	Clover Seed ..	12	2	0 ,,	16	00	,, cwt..	200	00		
,,	Corkwood	8 tons 5 cwt ,,			104	00	,, ton..	858	00		
,,	Barrel Staves ..	26 M.		,,	48	60	,, M. ..	1263	60		
,,	Bottles........	8½ gross,		,,	5	40	,, gross.	45	90		
,,	Wine	8 pipes port ,,			288	00	,, pipe..	2304	00		
	do.	4 do.		,, ,,	320	00	,, do.	1280	00		
	do.	36 doz.,		,, ,,	9	60	,, doz..	345	60		
	do.	73 ,,		,, ,,	9	00	,, do.	657	00		
	do.	109 ,, Cape ,,			4	20	,, do.	457	80		
	do.	3 p. Teneriff ,,			192	00	,, pipe..	576	00		
	do.	4 ,, Lisbon ,,			232	00	,, do.	928	00		
	do.	5 bts Sherry ,,			252	00	,, bt. ..	1260	00		
		Carried forward								12076	25

SIXTH SET.

TORONTO, 1st JANUARY, 1868.

J.F.		$	c.
	Brought forward..................	12076	25
	Debts due to me,—		
1	Reford & Dillon, Wellington St...$169 00		
„	Chas. Moore & Co., Wellington St. 290 00		
		459	00
1	Bills Receivable,—		
„	John Wilson's accept., due 23rd ...$140 00		
„	E. & J. Kelly's, „ „ 15th Feb 225 60		
„	John Harding's, „ „ 4th Mar. 71 40		
„	Steph. Delacour's, „ „ 17th „ 200 00		
		637	00
1	Cash on hand.................................	650	00
„	Warehouse and Stores, valued at............	4800	00
		18622	25

The above inventory of my property must be posted in the Ledger, in the Cr. side of the Stock Account, and in the Dr. side of each of the separate articles of goods, and each of the persons who owes me money, also of the Bills Receivable, the Cash, and the Warehouse and Stores. In Journalizing, therefore, say,—

CR.   STOCK.

	$	c.	$	c.
By Alum...........................	21	70		
„ Copperas......................	26	45		
„ &c., &c., &c...................				
„ Reford & Dillon...............	169	00		
„ &c., &c., &c...................				
„ Bills Receivable...............	637	00		
„ Cash............................	650	00		
„ Warehouse and Stores.........	4800	00		

BOOK-KEEPING.

TORONTO, 1st JANUARY, 1868.

J. F.			$	C.
	Debts due by me,—			
1	To John Boyd & Co., Front St...$ 409 30			
,,	,, Morrison, Taylor & Co., Wellington St...................... 229 85			
,,	,, Glynn, Mills & Co., London, Eng 151 80			
			790	95
1	List of Bills Payable,—			
,,	My Promissory Note to Nathaniel Low, at one day's date, payable with interest............$4000 00			
,,	My Acceptance of Johnstone & Co., 19th Jan'y............... 145 05			
,,	,, Acceptance to McDonnel & Co., 4th March............... 688 65			
,,	,, Acceptance to Wm. Murray, 13th April.................... 72 80			
			4906	50
			5697	45

These are debts due by me, partly in the form of Bills Payable, and partly in the form of Balances against me with persons with whom I have accounts   They must be put to the Dr. side of Stock, so that were the Stock balanced, the difference between the two sides would be my net property.   In Journalizing, therefore, say Stock Dr. to John Boyd & Co., etc., etc., and to Bills Payable.*

---

* NOTE.—After having carried these Accounts to the Journal in this manner, open an account for each of them in the Ledger, and not wait for the transactions which follow. This is what is called opening the Books.

W. R. ORR.

SIXTH SET.

TORONTO, 1st JANUARY, 1868.

J. F.		$	c.
2	Received from Antonia Silva & Co., St. Ubes, invoice of Salt, shipped per the "Active," 33 tons, at $20	660	00
	An invoice is a notice of goods sent off to me, stating the kind, quantity and value. As soon as they are sent off to me they are mine. I therefore say: Salt Dr. to Antonia Silva & Co., because the Salt came in, and I owe Antonia Silva & Co. for it.		
	——————— 2 ———————		
2	Bought of George Michie & Co., Front Street, for 3 months' Bill, 70 barrels Lochfine Herrings, at $4	280	00
	This and the two following transactions are purchases of goods on credit, we therefore make the different descriptions of goods Dr. to the persons from whom they were purchased.		
	——————— 3 ———————		
2	Bought of W. G. Taylor, London, England, 31 days, 4 cases Leghorn Hats, per list	2940	00
	Freight and Charges paid by him	139	20
	Commission for purchasing, 2 per cent.	58	80
		3138	
	——————— 4 ———————		
2	Bought of Smith & Arthurs, Wellington Street, 3 puncheons of Irish Whiskey, Nos. 1 to 3, 168 gallons, at $1.10	184	80
	Storage charged thereon	4	20
		189	00
	——————— 4 ———————		
2	Paid duty on 1 pun. Irish Whiskey, 56 gals., at 60 c $33 60		
	Permit and Officer's fees .... 1 '35		
		34	95
	These are expenses adding to the cost of the Whiskey. Irish Whiskey, therefore, is made Dr. to Cash.		

BOOK-KEEPING.

TORONTO, 6TH JANUARY, 1868.

J. F.		$	C.
2	Sold F. & G. Perkins & Co., Front Street,— 1 pun. Irish Whiskey, 56 gals., at $1.85 ..	103	60
	——————— 6 ———————		
2	Sold Hugh Miller, King Street,— 1 case Opium, 16½ lbs., at $2.90 per lb. ...	47	85
	——————— 7 ———————		
2	Sold for Cash to Edward Grant,— 3 doz. Cape Wine, at $4.50 per doz. ...... 3 doz. bottles under 50 „ „	13 1	50 50
		15	00
	This is a sale for Cash. The Cash came in, it is therefore Dr. The Wine went out, it is Cr. ; and Edward Grant's name does not appear in the Ledger so far as this transaction is concerned. He should, however, be mentioned in the Journal,* thus : Cash Dr. to Wine, Sold Edward Grant for Cash. The bottles here go along with the Wine, having been so entered in the inventory ; this is indicated by the word under. Had the bottles been empty, they would have been entered to the Cr. of the Bottle Account.		
	——————— 7 ———————		
2	Received from Reford & Dillon, Wellington Street,— 4 casks Brandy, at $266	1064	00

* In this, as in all other cases, it is not necessary to enter Grant's name in the Journal, as he paid Cash for the goods; it is sufficient that his name appear in the record of the transaction in the Day Book.

W. R. ORR.

SIXTH SET.

TORONTO, 7TH JANUARY, 1868.

J.F.		$	c.
2	Accepted Antonia Silva & Co.'s (St. Ubes) draft at 4 months from 20th December, due 23rd April, in London......................	660	00
	To accept a Bill or Draft is to put my name upon it, obliging myself to pay it ; Antonia Silva, therefore, is thus paid by a Bill Payable. The draft having been accepted by my signature, went out ; it is therefore Cr., and Antonia Silva Dr. I say, therefore, Antonia Silva Dr. to Bills Payable.		
	———————— 7 ————————		
2	Paid duty on 2 puncheons Irish Whiskey, 112 gals., at 60 c............................... Permit and Officer's fees......................	67 2	20 65
		69	85
	———————— 9 ————————		
3	Sold to Smith & Arthurs, (Wellington St.,) 1 pun. Irish Whiskey, 56 gals., at $1.90......	106	40
	———————— 9 ————————		
3	Received of F. & G. Perkins & Co., Front St., on account...	200	00
	———————— 10 ————————		
3	Paid duty on Salt, per the "Active" .... Landing and Charges ..'.....................	19 1	80 10
		20	90
	———————— 10 ————————		
3	Paid Freight and Charges on Leghorn Hats...	28	10
	———————— 11 ————————		
3	Sold Morrison, Taylor & Co., Front Street,— 6 M. barrel Staves, at $60	360	00

BOOK-KEEPING.

TORONTO, 11TH JANUARY, 1868.

J.F.		$	c.
3	Received of Hugh Miller, (King Street,) Finlay & Co.'s acceptance at 31 days.........	40	00
	Cash in full of Opium............................	7	85
		47	85
	Hugh Miller here pays me partly in a Bill Receivable, and partly in Cash. The Bill and the Cash came in, therefore they are each Dr. to Hugh Miller.		

_____ 12 _____

3	Sold J. E. Smith & Co., (Church St.,) at 2 months,—		
	2 pipes of P. Wine, at $336.00... $672 00		
	19 doz. Cape do., " 4.60... 87 40		
	19 " bottles under " 50... 9 50		
	8½ gross empty bottles, at 6.00... 51 00		
		819	90
	(See entry on 7th, respecting bottles.)		

_____ 13 _____

| 3 | Bought of Chas. Moore & Co., Wellington Street, at 4 months, 75 barrels Pot Ashes, per invoice, at $18.60 per bbl................. | 1395 | 00 |

_____ 13 _____

| 3 | Sold John Boyd & Co., (Front St.,) at 2½ per cent. for Cash, 14½ cwt. Copperas, at $1.30 .... | 18 | 85 |
| | As John Boyd & Co. did not pay Cash for this they are charged with the whole amount, if they had paid Cash the 2½ per cent. would have been entered and deducted.—W. R. O. | | |

_____ 14 _____

| 3 | Accepted Reford & Dillon's (Wellington St.) draft at 90 days, due 10th April......... | 1064 | 00 |

SIXTH SET.

TORONTO, 14TH JANUARY, 1868.

J.F.		$	C.
4	Accepted Smith & Arthur's (Wellington St.) draft, at 2 months, due 16th March.........	189	00
	───────────── 15 ─────────────		
4	Paid George Michie & Co., Front Street, Delacour's Acceptance................. $200 Cash in full of Herrings............... 80	280	00
	I owed George Michie & Co. $280, and having Delacour's acceptance, or Bill Receivable, as stated in the Inventory of my property, I gave that in part payment, and gave Cash for the remainder. I therefore say, George Michie & Co. Dr. to Bills Receivable and to Cash.		
	───────────── 16 ─────────────		
4	Sold for Cash to Mendicity Institution, 20 bbls. Herrings, at $5......................	100	00
	───────────── 16 ─────────────		
4	Sold for Cash to A. Macarthur, 12 lbs. Nut Galls, at 53 c.................................	6	36
	───────────── 17 ─────────────		
4	Sold Morrison, Taylor & Co. (Front St.) 61 days, 12 tons St. Ubes Salt, at $25............	300	00
	───────────── 17 ─────────────		
4	Sold John Boyd & Co. (Front St.) at 2½ per cent. for Cash,— 5 cwt. Alum, at $ 2.60 ...... $ 13 00 10 M. Staves, „ 60.00 ...... 600 00 3 cwt. Cloverseed, „ 20.00 ...... 60 00	673	00

G

BOOK-KEEPING.

TORONTO, 17TH JANUARY, 1868.

J.F.		$	c.
4	Received of Morrison, Taylor & Co., Front Street, in payment of Salt, J. Tottenham's note, due 4th February..................$160 Cash .... 137 Discount, 2 months' Interest............ 3	300	00
	This Salt was sold for the $300, but not to be paid for two months. (See former entry.) Morrison, Taylor & Co. offer to pay me immediately, if I will allow them interest for their money for two months, and take as part of it a Bill due in about a fortnight, which I agree to. I therefore Cr. Morrison, Taylor & Co. by the Bill Receivable, by Cash, and by the Discount, which three items make up the whole sum.		
	─────────17──────────		
4	Received of Morrison, Taylor & Co., Front Street, Cash on account........................	80	00
	─────────19──────────		
4	Remitted W. G. Taylor (London, Eng.,) on account of Leghorn Hats, my note, payable at Glynn, Mills & Co., 31 days...............	2000	00
	I owe W. G. Taylor money, and I draw a promissory note, binding myself to pay him $2000 in 31 days, which I send him. This is a Bill Payable, I therefore make him Dr. to Bills Payable.		
	─────────19──────────		
5	Paid my acceptance to Johnstone & Co., due this day...	145	05
	This acceptance is one of the Bills Payable, mentioned in the inventory of my property. It became due, and I paid Cash for it. The Cash goes out, it is therefore Cr.; the Bill comes in, it is Dr. I say Bills Payable Dr. to Cash.		

SIXTH SET.

TORONTO, 21st JANUARY, 1868.

J.F.		$	C.
5	Paid Saml. Booth, Adelaide Street, for Alterations made in Store, per agreement............	60	00
	———— 23 ————		
5	Sold Morrison, Taylor & Co., Front Street, for 3 months' bill,— 12 bbls. Pot ashes, at $ 7.00 ...... $ 84 00 15 „ Herrings, „ 5.20 ...... 78 00 10 M. Staves, „ 60.00 ...... 600 00 10 tons Salt, „ 25.00 ...... 250 00	1012	00
	———— 23 ————		
5	Sold for Cash to Lyman, Elliott & Co., King Street,— 40 lbs. Opium, at $2.60 ...... $104 00 50 „ Galls, „ 55 ...... 27 50 8½ cwt. Copperas, „ 2.00 ...... 17 00 1 cask Brandy, „ 348 00	496	50
	———— 24 ————		
5	Sold J. E. Smith & Co. (Church Street,) at 3 months,— 1 cask French Brandy............$ 350 90 1 hhd. Sugar, 1200 lbs., at 9 c... 108 00 3 pipes Port Wine, at $340.00... 1020 00 30 doz. Cape „ „ 4.30... 129 00	1607	90

BOOK-KEEPING.

TORONTO, 25TH JANUARY, 1868.

J.F.		$	C.
5	Drawn on J. E. Smith & Co. (Church St.,) in favor of Reford & Dillon (Wellington St.,) at 31 days............$1128 00 Discount allowed by Reford & Dillon, for prompt payment...... 10 00	1138	00
	I owe money to Reford & Dillon; J. E. Smith & Co. owe me money; I therefore draw a bill on J. E. Smith & Co., in favor of Reford & Dillon, which is in effect a direction to J. E. Smith & Co. to pay the money to Reford & Dillon on my account. But I thus pay Reford & Dillon before the money was due, and they allow me discount for prompt payment. If this transaction was entered fully, I should make Bills Receivable Dr. to J. E. Smith & Co., and Reford & Dillon Dr. to Bills Receivable; but the usual method is to make Reford & Dillon Dr. to J. E. Smith & Co., by which the two entries on the Bills Receivable account are avoided.		
	———— 25 ————		
5	Remitted Glynn, Mills & Co., (London, Eng.) Thos. Hodgen's draft on Hilton & Co., at 61 days, bought of Royal Canadian Bank...	800	00
	I wish to remit money to Glynn, Mills & Co., London. I therefore go to a broker or to the Exchange and purchase a Bill, payable in London, for the amount. To enter this fully, I should first say, Bills Receivable Dr. to Cash, and then Glynn, Mills & Co. Dr. to Bills Receivable. The usual mode, however, is to regard the Bill sent as Cash, and say, Glynn, Mills & Co. Dr. to Cash.		

TORONTO, 25TH JANUARY, 1868.

J. F.		$	C.
6	Paid Rent of Warehouse for last month..........	30	00
	This and the following entry, being payments of money, without any direct return, or any other person being chargeable with them, may either be put to the Dr. of Profit and Loss, or if I wish to keep a separate account of such charges, I may open an account for Warehouse rent and charges, and make that account Dr. The effect is the same, for that and similar accounts of expenses must come into the Profit and Loss account, before the Books are balanced.		
	———————29———————		
6	Paid Postage Account......................$ 6 70 Twine, Ropes, and Packing cases... 16 60 Clerk's Salary........................... 20 00 Porter's Wages........................... 6 40	49	70
	———————29———————		
6	Received Invoice from Reford & Dillon, Wellington Street, of Pearl Ashes shipped from Goderich, per Grand Trunk, 100 bbls., at $17.50.....	1750	00
	———————29———————		
6	Deficiency in settling Cash, supposed lost......	3	05
	Here the Cash went out, it is therefore Cr. ; but as it was lost, it is credited by Profit and Loss, say, Profit and Loss Dr. to Cash.		
	———————29———————		
6	Sold John Boyd & Co., (Front St.) 50 bbls. Pearl Ashes, now on their way from Goderich, deliverable 3 days after arrival, at $20 per bbl...........................	1000	00

BOOK-KEEPING.

TORONTO, 30TH JANUARY, 1868.

J. F.		$	C.
6	Received from John Boyd & Co. (Front St.)		
	J. Wilson's note, 4th March......$ 62 00		
	Wm. Kelly & Son's acceptance, 3rd		
	April 400 00		
	Thos. Hodgen's acceptance, 11th		
	April 150 00		
	E. Carpenter's note, 20th April... 100 00		
	———	712	00
	Cash on account of Ashes.....................	88	00
	Discount allowed, 2 months' interest on Cash.		90
		800	90
	John Boyd & Co. owe me money, they pay me in part with Bills on the persons mentioned, partly in Cash, and I allow them interest for the Cash, because it was paid before it was due; therefore John Boyd & Co. Cr. by Bills Receivable, by Cash, and by Discount.		
	———————31———————		
6	Discounted at Royal Canadian Bank,—		
	E. & J. Kelly's acceptance, 15th		
	February $225 60		
	John Harding's acceptance, 4th		
	March 71 40		
	John Tottenham's acceptance, 4th		
	February......................... 160 00		
	Wm. Kelly & Son's acceptance,		
	3rd April......................... 400 00		
	857 00		
	Interest per docket.................... 8 12		
		848	88
	I have these Bills in my possession, which are not yet due; but I want the money immediately. I therefore take them to a Banker, who gives me the money, deducting the interest for the time they have to run. The Bills went out; therefore Bills Receivable is Cr. first by the Cash received for them, and secondly by the Discount or Interest.		
	(NOTE.—Perhaps the more general practice now is to Dr. Cash Account with the full amount of the Bill Receivable, and Cr. the Bills Receivable Account by Cash for the like amount; then Cr. Cash by the Discount, and Dr. the Discount Account to Cash.—W. R. O.)		

SIXTH SET.

TORONTO, 31st JANUARY, 1868.

J. F.		$	C.
6	Remitted Glynn, Mills & Co., (London, Eng.) James Hamilton's draft on Jones, Lloyd & Co...,.................................$840 00 Discount ½ per cent. received...... 4 20		
		835	80
	Having occasion to remit money to Glynn, Mills & Co., London, I purchase a Bill on Jones, Lloyd & Co., London, for $840, but I pay only $835.80 for it. I may either make, first, Bills Receivable Dr. to Cash and to Discount, and then make Glynn, Mills & Co. Dr. to Bills Receivable for the whole sum ; or I may make Glynn, Mills & Co. Dr. to Cash and to Discount, and not enter the Bill in the account of Bills Receivable.		
	————————31—————————		
7	Received payment of John Wilson's acceptance, due 23rd inst............................	140	00
	This was a Bill in my possession, which, after falling due, was paid ; the Cash came in, it is therefore Dr., and the Bill went out, Cash is Dr. to Bills Receivable.		

BOOK-KEEPING.

TORONTO, 31st JANUARY, 1868.

J. F.		$	C.
7	Error in charging Morrison, Taylor.& Co., Front St., Pot Ashes, 23rd Jan., 12 bbls. at $7, instead of $19, say $12 per bbl......	144	00
	In this entry an error has been detected in the Books, and the mode of correcting errors is not to make erasures, but to make additional entries of an opposite kind. In this entry, goods sold had, by mistake, been charged too little; the person who bought them must, therefore be made Dr. to the kind of goods bought by him, for the amount of the error.		
	————————31————————		
7	Drawn on J. E. Smith & Co. (Church St.) in favor of W. G. Taylor, London, Eng., at 31 days, for.........................$1128 00 Discount allowed for prompt payment.. 10 00	1138	00
	(See a similar entry on January 25.)		
	————————31————————		
7	Error discovered in placing to the account of Smith & Arthurs, Wellington Street, 1 pun. Irish Whiskey, sold to F. G. Perkins & Co., Front Street, on Jan. 9th......................	106	40
	When one person is thus by mistake debited instead of another, Cr. the person so charged, by Error, and Dr. the person who ought to have been debited, To the goods sold him. The only alteration in the Real Account credited is, to draw the pen through the name of the person erroneously entered, and to write over it the name of the proper person. The amount in the money column remains unaltered.		

SIXTH SET.

TORONTO, 31ST, JANUARY, 1868.

J. F.		$	c.
7	Error in giving credit to Morrison, Taylor & Co., Front Street, for Cash paid by John Boyd & Co., Front Street, on 17th January	80	00
	This error is similar to the last, and must be corrected in a similar manner. Enter on the Dr. side of Morrison, Taylor & Co.'s account, To Error, and Cr. John Boyd & Co. By Cash. On the entry on the Cash Account, draw the pen through the name of Morrison, Taylor & Co., and write John Boyd & Co. over it.		

———————————31———————————

Inventory of Goods on hand,—

		Ts. cwt. qr. lbs.				$	c.
8	Alum......	2 3 0	@ $	2 80 ⅌ cwt.		7	70
,,	Tobacco ..	12 0 5	,,	1 20 ,, lb..		1446	00
,,	Opium	16¼	,,	2 45 ,, do..		40	42½
,,	Galls......	84	,,	50 ,, do..		42	00
,,	Cloverseed .	9 2 0	,,	16 00 ,, cwt.		152	00
,,	Corkwood . 8	5 0 0	,,	104 00 ,, ton.		858	00
,,	Wine, 6 pipes Port,		,,	288 00 ,, pipe		1728	00
,,	Do. 1 do. do.		,,	320 00 ,, do..		320	00
,,	Do. 73 doz. do.		,,	9 00 ,, doz.		657	00
,,	Do. 36 do. do.		,,	9 60 ,, do..		345	60
,,	Do. 57 do. do.		,,	4 20 ,, do..		239	40
,,	Do. 3 pipes Teneriffe,		,,	192 00 ,, pipe		576	00
,,	Do. 4 do. Lisbon,		,,	232 00 ,, do..		928	00
,,	Do. 5 butts Sherry,		,,	252 00 ,, butt		1260	00
,,	Salt, 11 tons,		,,	20 63 ,, ton.		226	93
,,	Herrings, 35 bbls.,		,,	4 00 ,, bbl.		140	00
,,	Leghorn Hats, 4 cases,		,,	791 52¼ each.		3166	10
,,	Irish Whiskey, 56 gals.,		,,	1 75 ⅌ gal.		98	00
,,	Brandy, 2 casks,		,,	266 00 each.		532	00
,,	Ashes, 63 bbls.,		,,	18 60 do.		1171	80
,,	Do. 50 do.		,,	17 50 do.		875	00
				Carried forward		14809	95½

BOOK-KEEPING.

TORONTO, 31ST JANUARY, 1868.

J.F.		$	C.
	Brought forward..........................	14809	95½
8	Bills Receivable on hand,—		
„	Finlay & Co.'s acceptance..........$ 40 00		
„	James Wilson's note, 4th March... 62 00		
„	Thos. Hodgen's do. 11th April... 150 00		
„	E. Carpenter's do. 20th do. ... 100 00		
		352	00
„	Cash on hand..	612	19
„	Warehouse and Stores, valued at................	4860	00
		20634	14½

This is an inventory taken as a preparation for balancing the books, Balance is made Dr. to all goods, and property of every description, remaining in my possession. The property in this case consists of the various kinds of Goods enumerated, of Cash, of Warehouse, of Bills Receivable, and of debts due to me. Each description of goods for which an account has been opened is credited, By Balance, for the quantity and value on hand; also Cash for the Cash on hand; and Warehouse and Stores, for the value of them; Bills Receivable, for the whole amount of Bills in one sum; and persons, for the sums due respectively by them.

8	List of debts due to me,—		
„	F. & G. Perkins & Co...............$ 10 00		
„	Morrison, Taylor & Co............ 1286 15		
„	John Boyd & Co...................... 401 65		
„	J. E. Smith & Co................... 171 80		
„	Glyhn, Mills & Co................. 1488 20		
		3357	80
		23991	94½

SIXTH SET.

TORONTO, 31ST JANUARY, 1868.

J.F.			$	c.
8	List of debts due by me,—			
„	Reford & Dillon..................$ 443 00			
„	Chas. Moore & Co.................. 1105 00			
			1548	00
„	List of Bills Payable,—			
„	My Note to N. Low, 1 day's date.$4000 00			
„	Accept. to M. Donnell & Co. 4th Mar. 688 65			
„	Do. „ Wm. Murray, 13th April. 72 80			
„	Do. „ A. Silva & Co., 23rd do. 660 00			
„	Do. „ Reford & Dillon, 10th do. 1064 00			
„	Do. „ Smith & Arthurs, 16 Mar. 189 00			
„	Do. „ W. G. Taylor, 22nd Feb. 2000 00			
			8674	45
			10222	45

From my property must be deducted debts due by me. This is done by making them Dr. to Balance. The debts here are balances of accounts not settled, and Bills Payable. Balance is made Cr. by each of the persons to whom I owe money; or, what is the same thing, each person is made Dr. to Balance for the amount of what I owe him, and Bills Payable are made Dr. in one sum for all such bills still remaining unpaid.

BOOK-KEEPING.

TORONTO, 31ST JANUARY, 1868.

The Journal being written according to the directions given, the Ledger must be posted from it. Then, before entering the Balance of the Goods, &c., on hand, according to the Inventory, make the trial balance. Enter then, from the Inventory, the Balances of Goods on hand to the Cr. side of each account; this ought to agree with the balance found by comparing the quantities on each side, as in Set 3.* Proceed to balance and close the Cash Account and Personal Accounts, the difference between the two sides being entered, To or By Balance.† Close the Real Accounts by entering the difference between the two sides, To or By Profit and Loss. Close also, in the same manner, the accounts of Discount or Interest, Charges, &c. Collect now all the balances upon a separate sheet of paper, ruled like the Ledger, as directed in former sets; and whenever the Balance is entered on the Dr. side, to make the sides equal, enter it on the Cr. side of the Balance Sheet, and *vice versa*. Proceed now to close the Profit and Loss Account. Enter in the difference between the two sides, To or By Stock for my gain or loss, as the case may be, and write the same sum on the opposite side of the Stock Account, To or By Profit and Loss. Close now the Balance Account, entering the difference, To or By Stock for my net estate, entering the same sum on the opposite side of the Stock Account, To or By Balance. The two sides of the Stock Account should now be equal, which closes the books; if the sides be not equal, an error has been committed, which must be searched out and corrected.

---

* I have not carried the quantities of Goods to their respective accounts in this set; a Stock Book should be kept, in which to enter the Goods on hand, and those bought and sold.

† Not To Balance—so far as the Cash Account is concerned—See former note, page 8.

W. R. ORR.

Sixth Set—Questions.

QUESTIONS ON THE SIXTH SET.

Of what accounts are there examples given in this set? In journalizing, for what do you debit and credit Stock? When goods come in, are they Dr. or Cr.? What are Bills Receivable, and Bills Payable? When you receive a Bill Receivable in payment of goods, how would you enter it? When are goods Dr. to Bills Payable? When to Bills Receivable? What if the Bill was received from a person, with whom you have an account towards that account? What if a Bill Receivable is paid to a person with whom you have credit? What is done when a Bill is purchased for Cash to be remitted? What is done when one person's acceptance is paid to another, with both of whom you have accounts? What do you mean by getting Bills discounted? What is done when a person pays an account partly in Cash, and partly in Bills? How are transactions traced from one book to another?

SIXTH SET.

REAL ACCOUNTS SUBDIVIDED INTO VARIOUS KINDS OF GOODS;

ALSO OF

TRANSACTIONS BY BILLS, WITH DISCOUNT, INTEREST, &c.,

FIRST.

EACH TRANSACTION SEPARATELY JOURNALIZED.

N. B.—This Set of books being of the greatest value to the learner, as its transactions are of a varied and practical nature, more so than any set in any author I have ever seen. I have journalized and posted the transactions according to the original, viz: each transaction separately.

I have then made out separate books for each kind of transaction, viz: Cash Book, and Bills Receivable and Payable Books, in which are collected all the transactions in Cash and Bills, and have entered the Credit transactions only in the Day Book. (It will be understood that in this case I use the original entries merely as a Waste Book).* I then collect from the various books all the transactions into the Journal.

---

* All the transactions should be transferred to a Waste Book prepared by the pupil, before proceeding with this Set by the collected method; He should also prepare his Cash Book and Bill Books, also a Cash Book and Waste Book for the Fifth Set, Single Entry. And as he transfers the entries from the newly made-out blotter, he should enter in the margin the initials representing the names of the Subsidiary books into which he has taken the respective entries —thus: C. B. (Cash Book), D. B. (Day Book), B. R. (Bills Receivable), B. P. (Bills Payable), of course the folio No. of these books should be entered as usual in the column for that purpose in the Blotter or Waste Book.

W. R. ORR.

Book-keeping—Sixth Set.

This form will give the learner an insight into the mode pursued by some of the best wholesale houses, and is adopted and recommended as the best method by Morrison and others; but daily posting is perhaps, after all, the easiest and surest.

W. R. ORR.

JOURNAL.

TORONTO, 1st JANUARY, 1868.

L.F.			P.D.B	$	C.	$	C.
1	Cr. Stock,—		68				
,,	By Alum		,,	21	70		
,,	,, Copperas		,,	26	45		
,,	,, Tobacco		,,	1485	60		
2	,, Sugar		,,	114	75		
,,	,, Opium		,,	178	85		
,,	,, Galls		,,	73	00		
,,	,, Cloverseed		,,	200	00		
3	,, Corkwood		,,	858	00		
,,	,, Barrel Staves		,,	1263	60		
,,	,, Bottles		,,	45	90		
,,	,, Wine		,,	7808	40		
4	,, Reford & Dillon, Wellington St..		69	169	00		
,,	,, Chas. Moore & Co., do.		,,	290	00		
,,	,, Bills Receivable		,,	637	00		
,,	,, Cash		,,	650	00		
5	,, Warehouse and Stores		,,	4800	00		
						18622	25
	——— 1 ———						
1	Dr. Stock,—		70				
5	To John Boyd & Co., Front St		,,	409	30		
,,	,, Morrison, Taylor & Co., do		,,	229	85		
,,	,, Glynn, Mills & Co., London, Eng.		,,	151	80		
						790	95
6	,, Bills Payable		,,			4906	50
						5697	45

Sixth Set—Journal.

FOL. 2

TORONTO, 2ND JANUARY, 1868.

L.F.		P.D.B	$	C.	$	C.
6	Cr. Antonia Silva & Co. St. Ubes	71				
6	By Salt..........................				660	00
	————— 2 —————					
6	Cr. George Michie & Co. Front St	71				
7	By Herrings...................				280	00
	————— 3 —————					
7	Cr. W. G. Taylor, London, Eng.	71				
7	By Leghorn Hats................				3138	00
	————— 4 —————					
8	Cr. Smith & Arthur, Wellington Street	71				
7	By Irish Whiskey................				189	00
	————— 4 —————					
7	Dr. Irish Whiskey,—	71				
4	To Cash paid duty.............				34	95
	————— 6 —————					
8	Dr. F. & G. Perkins & Co. Front-st.	72				
7	To Irish Whiskey..............				103	60
	————— 6 —————					
8	Dr. Hugh Miller, King-st.,—	72				
2	To Opium.....................				47	85
	————— 7 —————					
4	Dr. Cash,—	72				
3	To Wine sold E. Grant..........				15	00
	————— 7 —————					
4	Cr. Reford & Dillon, Wellington Street	72				
8	By Brandy.....................				1064	00
	————— 7 —————					
6	Dr. Antonia Silva & Co. St. Ubes	73				
6	To Bills Payable accepted their draft 23rd April................				660	00
	————— 7 —————					
7	Dr. Irish Whiskey,—	73				
4	To Cash paid duty.............				69	85

H

Sixth Set—Journal.

FOL. 3

TORONTO, 9TH JANUARY, 1868.

L.F.		P.D.B	$	C.	$	C.
8	Dr. Smith & Arthurs, *Wellington Street.*	73				
7	To Irish Whiskey..............				106	40
	———— 9 ————					
8	Cr. F. & G. Perkins & Co. Front-st.	73				
4	By Cash on account.............				200	00
	———— 10 ————					
6	Dr. Salt,—	73				
4	To Cash paid duty..............				20	90
	———— 10 ————					
7	Dr. Leghorn Hats,—	73				
4	To Cash paid Freights, &c.......				28	10
	———— 11 ————					
5	Dr. Morrison, Taylor & Co., *Front Street.*	73				
3	To Barrel Staves................				360	00
	———— 11 ————					
8	Cr. Hugh Miller, King Street.	74				
4	By Bills Receivable..............		40	00		
4	,, Cash.......................		7	85		
					47	85
	———— 12 ————					
9	Dr. J. E Smith & Co., Church-st.	74				
3	To Wine......................		768	90		
3	,, Bottles, 8½ gross............		51	00		
					819	90
	———— 13 ————					
4	Cr. Chas. Moore & Co., *Wellington Street.*	74				
9	By Potashes....................				1395	00
	———— 13 ————					
5	Dr. John Boyd & Co., Front-st.	74				
1	To Copperas...................				18	85
	———— 14 ————					
4	Dr. Reford & Dillon, *Wellington Street.*	74				
6	To Bills Payable..........				1064	00

Sixth Set—Journal.

FOL. 4

TORONTO, 14TH JANUARY, 1868.

L.F.		P.D.B	$	C.	$	C.
8	Dr. Smith & Arthurs,	75				
	Wellington Street.					
6	To Bills Payable...............				189	00
	———— 15 ————					
6	Dr. George Michie & Co.,	75				
	Front Street.					
4	To Bills Receivable............		200	00		
4	,, Cash		80	00		
					280	00
	———— 16 ————					
4	Dr. Cash,	75				
7	To Herrings...................				100	00
	———— 16 ————					
4	Dr. Cash,	75				
2	To Galls				6	36
	———— 17 ————					
5	Dr. Morrison, Taylor & Co.,	75				
	Front Street.					
6	To Salt				300	00
	———— 17 ————					
5	Dr. John Boyd & Co., Front-st.	75				
1	To Alum		13	00		
3	,, Barrel Staves...............		600	00		
2	,, Cloverseed		60	00		
					673	00
	———— 17 ————					
5	Cr. Morrison, Taylor & Co.,	76				
	Front Street.					
4	By Bills Receivable............		160	00		
4	,, Cash		137	00		
9	,, Discount...................		3	00		
					300	00
	———— 17 ————					
5	Cr. Morrison, Taylor & Co., .	76				
	Front Street.					
10	By Cash on account				80	00
	———— 19 ————					
7	Dr. W. G. Taylor, London, Eng.	76				
6	To Bills Payable...............				2000	00

Sixth Set—Journal.

FOL. 5

TORONTO, 19TH JANUARY, 1868.

L..F.		P.D.11	$	C.	$	C.
6	Dr. Bills Payable,—	76				
10	To Cash, paid my acceptance to Johnstone & Co.............				145	05
	——————— 21 ———————					
5	To Warehouse & Store,—	76				
10	To Cash for alterations.........				60	00
	——————— 23 ———————					
5	Dr. Morrison, Taylor & Co., Front Street.	77				
9	To Potashes...................		84	00		
7	,, Herrings...................		78	00		
3	,, Barrel Staves..............		600	00		
6	,, Salt		250	00		
					1012	00
	——————— 23 ———————					
10	Dr. Cash,—	77				
2	To Opium.....................		104	00		
2	,, Galls		27	50		
1	,, Copperas		17	00		
8	,, Brandy		348	00		
					496	50
	——————— 24 ———————					
9	Dr. J. E. Smith & Co. Church-st.	77				
8	To Brandy		350	90		
2	,, Sugar.....................		108	00		
3	,, Wine		1149	00		
					1607	90
	——————— 25 ———————					
4	Dr. Reford & Dillon, Wellington Street.	78				
9	To J. E. Smith & Co., Church-st., for his acceptance 31 days....		1128	00		
9	,, Discount in full.............		10	00		
					1138	00
	——————— 25 ———————					
5	Dr. Glynn, Mills & Co., London, Eng.	78				
10	To Cash paid for Hodgen's draft on Hilton & Co., 61 days......				800	00

Sixth Set—Journal.

FOL. 6

TORONTO, 25TH JANUARY, 1868.

L.F.		P.D.B	$	C.	$	C.
9	Dr. Rent and Charges,—	79				
10	To Cash paid rent of Warehouse ..				30	00
	——————— 29 ———————					
9	Dr. Rent and Charges,—	79				
10	To Cash paid postage, twine, packing cases, etc.		23	30		
10	,, Cash, paid Clerk and Porter's wages		26	40		
					49	70
	——————— 29 ———————					
4	Cr. Reford & Dillon,	79				
	Wellington Street.					
9	By Ashes				1750	00
	——————— 29 ———————					
10	Dr. Profit and Loss,—	79				
10	To Cash, supposed lost				3	05
	——————— 29 ———————					
5	Dr. John Boyd & Co., Front-st.	79				
9	To Ashes				1000	00
	——————— 30 ———————					
5	Cr. John Boyd & Co., Front-st.	80				
4	By Bills Receivable		712	00		
10	,, Cash......................		88	00		
9	,, Discount		00	90		
					800	90
	——————— 31 ———————					
4	Cr. Bills Receivable,—	80				
10	By Cash for four bills............		848	88		
9	,, Discount for Interest..........		8	12		
					857	00
	——————— 31 ———————					
5	Dr. Glynn, Mills & Co.,	81				
	London, Eng.					
10	To Cash paid for Draft..........		835	80		
9	,, Discount received............		4	20		
					840	00

Sixth Set—Journal.

Fol. 7

TORONTO, 31ST JANUARY, 1868.

L..F.		P.D.B	$	c.	$	c.
10	Dr. Cash,—	81				
4	To Bills Receivable, received payment of Wilsons acceptance....				140	00
	————— 31 —————					
5	Dr. Morrison, Taylor & Co.,	82				
	Front Street.					
9	To Ashes, for error in charging 12 brls, at $7.00 instead of $19.00 23rd January				144	00
	————— 31 —————					
7	Dr. W. G. Taylor, London, Eng	82				
9	To J. E. Smith & Co., Church-st., for their acceptance 31 days..		1128	00		
9	,, Discount in full..............		10	00		
					1138	00
	————— 31 —————					
8	Cr. Smith & Arthur,	82				
	Wellington Street.					
8	By F. & G. Perkins, for 1 pun. Irish Whiskey charged them in error 9th January				106	40
	————— 31 —————					
5	Cr. John Boyd & Co. Front-st.	83				
5	By Morrison, Taylor & Co., Front Street, for Cash credited in error				80	00

Sixth Set—Journal.

FOL. 8

TORONTO, 31ST JANUARY, 1868.

L.F.		P.D.B	$	C.	$	C.
11	Dr. Balance,—	83				
1	To Alum .... 2 cwt. 3 qrs. 0 lbs.	,,	7	70		
1	,, Tobacco ..12 ,, 0 ,, 5 ,,	,,	1446	00		
2	,, Opium.... ,, ,, 16¼ ,,	,,	40	42½		
2	,, Galls .... ,, ,, 84 ,,	,,	42	00		
2	,, Cloverseed. 9 ,, 2 ,, 0 ,,	,,	152	00		
3	,, Corkwood, 8 tons 5 cwt 0 qrs 0 lbs	,,	858	00		
3	,, Wine, 19 pipes, 166 doz.	,,	6054	00		
6	,, Salt, 11 tons	,,	226	93		
7	,, Herrings, 35 bbls.	,,	140	00		
7	,, Leghorn Hats, 4 cases	,,	3166	10		
7	,, Irish Whiskey, 56 gals.........	,,	98	00		
8	,, Brandy, 2 casks	,,	532	00		
9	,, Ashes, 113 bbls.	,,	2046	80		
					14809	95½
4	,, Bills Receivable	84			352	00
10	,, Cash	,,			612	19
5	,, Warehouse and Store..........	,,			4860	00
8	,, F. & G. Perkins & Co.	,,	10	00		
5	,, Morrison, Taylor & Co	,,	1286	15		
5	,, John Boyd & Co	,,	401	65		
9	,, J. E. Smith & Co.	,,	171	80		
5	,, Glynn, Mills & Co	,,	1488	20		
					3357	80
					23991	94½
	──────── 31 ────────					
11	Cr. Balance,—	85				
4	By Reford & Dillon	,,	443	00		
4	,, Chas. Moore & Co	,,	1105	00		
					1548	00
6	,, Bills Payable	,,			8674	45
					10222	45

INDEX TO LEDGER.

SIXTH SET.

A

Alum	1
Ashes	9

B

Barrel Staves	3
Bottles	3
Bills Receivable	4
Boyd, John & Co., Front Street	5
Bills Payable	6
Brandy	8
Balance	11

C

Copperas	1
Cloverseed	2
Corkwood	3
Cash	4 10

D

Discount	9

G

Galls	2
Glynn, Mills & Co., London, Eng.	5

H

Herrings	7

I

Irish Whiskey	7

L

Leghorn Hats	7

M

Moore, Chas. & Co., Wellington St.	4
Morrison, Taylor & Co., Front St.	5
Michie, G. & Co., Front Street	6
Miller, H., King Street	8

O

Opium	2

P

Perkins, F. G. & Co., Front St.	8
Profit and Loss	10

R

Reford & Dillon, Wellington St.	4
Rent and Charges	9

S

Stock	1
Sugar	2
Silva, A. & Co., St. Ubes	6
Salt	6
Smith & Arthur, Wellington St.	8
Smith, J. E. & Co., Church St.	9

T

Tobacco	1
Taylor, W. G., London, England.	7

W

Wine	3
Warehouse and Stores	5

FOL.   FOL.
1   1

DR.   STOCK.   CR.

1868.			J.F	$	c.	1868.			J.F	$	c.
Jan.	1	To Sundries.	1	5697	45	Jan.	1	By Sundries ..	1	18622	25
			L.F						L.F		
,,	31	,, Balance.	11	13769	49½*	,,	31	,, Profit & Loss	10	844	69½
				19466	94½					19466	94½
						Feb.	1	By Balance ..		13769	49½

DR.   ALUM.   CR.

1868.			J.F	$	c.	1868.			J.F	$	c.
Jan.	1	To Stock	1	21	70	Jan.	17	By J.Boyd & Co	4	13	00
						,,	31	,, Balance ..	8	7	70
									L.F		
						,,	31	,, Profit & Loss	10	1	00
				21	70					21	70
Feb.	1	To Balance ..		7	70						

DR.   COPPERAS.   CR.

1868.			J.F	$	c.	1868.			J.F	$	c.
Jan.	1	To Stock	1	26	45	Jan.	13	By J.Boyd & Co	3	18	85
			L.F			,,	23	,, Cash......	5	17	00
,,	31	,, Profit & Loss	10	9	40						
				35	85					35	85

DR.   TOBACCO.   CR.

1868.			J.F	$	c.	1868.			J.F	$	c.
Jan.	1	To Stock	1	1485	60	Jan.	31	By Balance ..	8	1446	00
									L.F		
						,,	,,	,, Profit & Loss	10	39	60
				1485	60					1485	60
Feb.	1	To Balance ..		1446	00						

* Fractions of cents are not usually carried through the books in actual business, but as the ½ cent, in this case, occurred in calculating the balances on hand, I have allowed it to pass through the accounts, as it may serve the purpose of exemplifying, to the pupil, the exactness of the science. (See also Stock Account, Sixth Set collectedly.)   W. R. ORR.

Sixth Set—Ledger.

DR. SUGAR. CR.

1868.			J.F	$	C.	1868.			J.F	$	C.
Jan.	1	To Stock	1	114	75	Jan.	24	By J. E. Smith & Co	5	108	00
						,,	31	,, Profit & Loss	L.F 10	6	75
				114	75					114	75

DR. OPIUM. CR.

1868.			J.F	$	C.	1868.			J.F	$	C.
Jan.	1	To Stock	1	178	85	Jan.	6	By H. Miller..	2	47	85
,,	31	,, Profit & Loss	L.F 10	13	42½	,,	23	,, Cash......	5	104	00
						,,	31	,, Balance ..	8	40	42½
				192	27½					192	27½
Feb.	1	To Balance ..		40	42½						

DR. GALLS. CR.

1868.			J.F	$	C.	1868.			J.F	$	C.
Jan.	1	To Stock	1	73	00	Jan.	16	By Cash......	4	6	36
,,	31	,, Profit & Loss	L.F 10	2	86	,,	23	,, do.	5	27	50
						,,	31	,, Balance ..	8	42	00
				75	86					75	86
Feb.	1	To Balance ..		42	00						

DR. CLOVERSEED. CR.

1868.			J.F	$	C.	1868.			J.F	$	C.
Jan.	1	To Stock	1	200	00	Jan.	17	By J. Boyd & Co	4	60	00
,,	31	,, Profit & Loss	L.F 10	12	00	,,	31	,, Balance....	8	152	00
				212	00					212	00
Feb.	1	To Balance ..		152	00						

Sixth Set—Ledger.

CORKWOOD.

FOL. 3 DR.			J.F	$	c.	1868.			J.F	$	c.
1868.											
Jan.	1	To Stock	1	858	00	Jan.	31	By Balance ..	8	858	00
Feb.	1	To Balance ..		858	00						

BARREL STAVES.

DR.			J.F	$	c.	1868.	c.		J.F	$	c.
1868.											
Jan.	1	To Stock	1	1263	60	Jan.	11	By Morrison T. & Co	3	360	00
,,	31	,, Profit & Loss	L.F 10	296	40	,,	17	,, J. Boyd & Co	4	600	00
						,,	23	,, Morrison, T. & Co	5	600	00
				1560	00					1560	00

BOTTLES.

DR.			J.F	$	c.	1868.			J.F	$	c.
1868.											
Jan.	1	To Stock	1	45	90	Jan.	12	By J. E. Smith & Co......	3	51	00
,,	31	,, Profit & Loss	L.F 10	5	10						
				51	00					51	00

WINE.

DR.			J.F	$	c.	1868.			J.F	$	c.
1868.											
Jan.	1	To Stock	1	7808	40	Jan.	7	By Cash......	2	15	00
,,	31	,, Profit & Loss	L.F 10	178	50	,,	12	,, J. E. Smith & Co......	3	768	90
						,,	24	,, J. E. Smith & Co......	5	1149	00
						,,	31	,, Balance ..	8	6054	00
				7986	90					7986	90
Feb.	1	,, Balance ..		6054	00						

Sixth Set—Ledger.

FOL. 4

Dr.   REFORD & DILLON, Wellington-St.   Cr.   FOL. 4

1868.			J.F	$	c.	1868.			J.F	$	c.
Jan.	1	To Stock	1	169	00	Jan.	7	By Brandy	2	1064	00
,,	14	,, Bills Payable	3	1064	00	,,	29	,, Ashes	6	1750	00
,,	25	,, Sundries	5	1138	00						
,,	31	,, Balance	8	443	00						
				2814	00					2814	00
						Feb.	1	By Balance		443	00

Dr.   CHAS. MOORE & Co., Wellington-St.   Cr.

1868.			J.F	$	c.	1868.			J.F	$	c.
Jan.	1	To Stock	1	290	00	Jan.	13	By Ashes	3	1395	00
,,	31	,, Balance	8	1105	00						
				1395	00					1395	00
						Feb.	1	By Balance		1105	00

Dr.   BILLS RECEIVABLE.   Cr.

1868.			J.F	$	c.	1868.			J.F	$	c.
Jan.	1	To Stock	1	637	00	Jan.	14	By G. Michie & Co	4	200	00
,,	11	,, H. Miller	3	40	00	,,	30	,, Sundries	6	857	00
,,	17	,, Morrison, T. & Co	4	160	00	,,	,,	,, Cash	7	140	00
,,	30	,, J. Boyd & Co	6	712	00	,,	31	,, Balance	8	352	00
				1549	00					1549	00
Feb.	1	To Balance		352	00						

Dr.   CASH.   Cr.

1868.			J.F	$	c.	1868.			J.F	$	c.
Jan.	1	To Stock	1	650	00	Jan.	4	By Irish Whisky	2	34	95
,,	7	,, Wine	2	15	00	,,	7	,, do.	,,	69	85
,,	9	,, F. G. Perkins & Co	3	200	00	,,	10	,, Salt	3	20	90
,,	11	,, H. Miller	,,	7	85	,,	,,	,, Leghorn Hats	,,	28	10
,,	16	,, Herrings	4	100	00	,,	14	,, G. Michie & Co	4	80	00
,,	,,	,, Galls	,,	6	35						
,,	17	,, Morrison, T. & Co	,,	137	00						
			L.F						L.F		
		Carried forward	10	1116	21			Carried forward*	10	233	80

* Example of an account transferred to another Folio.

Sixth Set—Ledger.

FOL. 5   Dr.   WAREHOUSE & STORES.   Cr.   FOL. 5

1868.			J.F	$	c.	1868.			J.F	$	c.
Jan.	1	To Stock	1	4800	00	Jan.	31	By Balance ..	8	4860	00
,,	21	,, Cash......	5	60	00						
				4860	00					4860	00
Feb.	1	To Balance ..		4860	00						

Dr.   JOHN BOYD & Co., Front-St.   Cr.

1868.			J.F	$	c.	1868.			J.F	$	c.
Jan.	13	To Copperas..	3	18	85	Jan.	1	By Stock......	1	409	30
,,	17	,, Sundries ..	4	673	00	,,	30	,, Sundries....	6	800	90
,,	29	,, Ashes ..	6	1000	00	,,	31	Morrison, T & Co	7	80	00
						,,		,, Balance	L.F 8	401	65
				1691	85					1691	85
Feb.	1	To Balance ..		401	65						

Dr.   MORRISON, TAYLOR & Co., Front-St.   Cr.

1868.			J.F	$	c.	1868			J.F	$	c.
Jan.	11	To Barrel Staves	3	360	00	Jan.	1	By Stock	1	229	85
,,	17	,, Salt	4	300	00	,,	17	,, Sundries ..	4	300	00
,,	23	,, Sundries ..	5	1012	00	,,	,,	,, Cash......	4	80	00
,,	31	,, Ashes (error,	7	144	00	,,	31	,, Balance ..	8	1286	15
,,	,,	,, J. Boyd & Co	,,	80	00						
				1896	00					1896	00
Feb.	1	To Balance....		1286	15						

Dr.   GLYNN, MILLS & Co., London, Eng.   Cr.

1868.			J.F	$	c.	1868.			J.F	$	c,
Jan.	25	To Cash......	5	800	00	Jan.	1	By Stock	1	151	80
,,	31	,, Sundries ..	6	840	00	,,	31	,, Balance ..	8	1488	20
				1640	00					1640	00
Feb.	1	To Balance ..		1488	20						

Sixth Set—Ledger.

FOL. 6   DR.   BILLS PAYABLE.   CR.   FOL. 6

1868.			J.F	$	C.	1868.			J.F	$	C.
Jan.	19	To Cash	5	145	05	Jan.	1	By Stock	1	4906	50
,,	31	,, Balance ..	8	8674	45	,,	7	,, A. Silva & Co	2	660	00
						,,	13	,, Reford & Dillon	3	1064	00
						,,	14	,, Smith & Arthurs	4	189	00
						,,	19	,, W. G. Taylor	,,	2000	00
				8819	50					8819	50
						Feb.	1	By Balance ..		8674	45

DR.   ANTONIA, SILVA & Co., ST. UBES.   CR.

1868.			J.F	$	C.	1868.			J.F	$	C.
Jan.	7	To Bills Payable	2	660	00	Jan.	2	By Salt	2	660	00

DR.   SALT.   CR.

1868.			J.F	$	C.	1868.			J.F	$	C.
Jan.	2	To A. Silva & Co	2	660	00	Jan.	17	By Morrison, T. & Co....	4	300	00
,,	10	,, Cash	3	20	90	,,	23	,, Morrison, T. & Co....	5	250	00
,,	31	,, Profit & Loss	L.F 10	96	03	,,	31	,, Balance ..	8	226	93
				776	93					776	93
Feb.	1	To Balance....		226	93						

DR.   GEORGE MICHIE & Co., FRONT-ST.   CR.

1868.			J.F	$	C.	1868.			J.F	$	C.
Jan.	14	To Sundries...	4	280	00	Jan.	2	By Herrings ..	2	280	00

Sixth Set—Ledger.

FOL. 7   DR.   HERRINGS   CR.   FOL. 7

1868.		J.F	$	C.	1868.		J.F	$	C.
Jan.	2 To G. Michie & Co......	2	280	00	Jan.	16 By Cash	4	100	00
		L.F			,,	23 ,, Morrison, T. & Co....	5	78	00
,,	31 ,, Profit & Loss	10	38	00	,,	31 ,, Balance	8	140	00
			318	00				318	00
Feb.	1 To Balance....		140	00					

DR.   W. G. TAYLOR, LONDON, ENG.   CR.

1868.		J.F	$	C.	1868.		J.F	$	C.
Jan.	19 To Bills Payable	4	2000	00	Jan.	3 By Leghorn Hats	2	3138	00
,,	31 ,, J. E. Smith & Co....	7	1128	00					
,,	,, ,, Discount ..	,,	10	00					
			3138	00				3138	00

DR.   LEGHORN HATS.   CR.

1868.		J.F	$	C.	1868.		J.F	$	C.
Jan.	3 To W.G. Taylor	2	3138	00	Jan.	31 By Balance....	8	3166	10
,,	10 ,, Cash	3	28	10					
			3166	10				3166	10
Feb.	1 To Balance....		3166	10					

DR.   IRISH WHISKEY   CR.

1868.		J.F	$	C.	1868.		J.F	$	C.
Jan.	4 To Smith & Arthurs........	2	189	00	Jan.	6 By F. & G. Perkins	2	103	60
,,	,, ,, Cash........	2	34	95	,,	9 " Smith & Arthurs........	3	106	40
,,	7 ,, do.	,,	69	85	,,	31 ,, Balance....	8	98	00
		L.F							
,,	31 ,, Profit & Loss	10	14	20					
			308	00				308	00
Feb.	1 To Balance....	1	98	00					

Sixth Set—Ledger.

FOL. 8

DR.   SMITH & ARTHURS, WELLINGTON-ST.   CR.   FOL. 8

1868.			J.F.	$	c.	1868.			J.F.	$	c.
Jan.	9	To Irish Whisky	3	106	40	Jan.	9	By Irish Whisky	2	189	00
,,	14	,, Bills Payable	4	189	00	,,	31	,, F. G. Perkins & Co....	7	106	40
				295	40					295	40

DR.   F. & G. PERKINS & CO., FRONT-ST.   CR.

1868.			J.F.	$	c.	1868.			J.F.	$	c.
Jan.	6	To Irish Whisky	2	103	60	Jan.	9	By Cash.......	3	200	00
,,	31	,, Smith & Arthurs.......	7	106	40	,,	31	,, Balance....	8	10	00
				210	00					210	00
Feb.	1	To Balance....		10	00						

DR.   HUGH MILLER & CO., KING-ST.   CR.

1868.			J.F.	$	c.	1868.			J.F.	$	c.
Jan.	6	To Opium	2	47	85	Jan.	11	By Sundries....	3	47	85

DR.   BRANDY.   CR.

1868.			J.F.	$	c.	1868.			J.F.	$	c.
Jan.	7	To Reford & Dillon.........	2	1064	00	Jan.	23	By Cash......	5	348	00
			L.F				24	" J. E. Smith & Co.......	,,	350	90
,,	31	,, Profit & Loss	10	166	90	,,	31	" Balance....	8	532	00
				1230	90					1230	90
Feb.	1	To Balance....		532	00						

Sixth Set—Ledger.

FOL. 9   FOL. 9

Dr.   J. E. SMITH & Co., Church-St.   Cr.

1868.			J.F.	$	c.	1868.			J.F.	$	c.
Jan.	12	To Sundries....	3	819	90	Jan.	25	By Reford & Dillon...	5	1128	00
,,	24	,, do.	5	1607	90	,,	31	,, W.G. Taylor	7	1128	00
						,,	,,	,, Balance....	8	171	80
				2427	80					2427	80
Feb.	1	To Balance....		171	80						

Dr.   A S H E S.   Cr.

1868.			J.F.	$	c.	1868.			J.F.	$	c.
Jan.	13	ToC.Moore&Co	3	1395	00	Jan.	23	By Morrison, T. & Co......	5	84	00
,,	29	,, Reford & Dillon........	6	1750	00	,,	29	,, John Boyd & Co........	6	1000	00
,,	31	,, Profit & Loss	L.F 10	129	80	,,	31	,, Morrison, T. & Co......	7	144	00
						,,	,,	,, Balance	8	2046	80
				3274	80					3274	80
Feb.	1	To Balance....		2046	80						

Dr.   D I S C O U N T.   Cr.

1868.			J.F.	$	c.	1868.			J.F.	$	c.
Jan.	17	To Morrison, T. & Co.....	4	3	00	Jan.	25	By Reford & Dillon........	5	10	00
,,	30	,, J. Boyd&Co.	6		90	,,	31	,, Glynn, Mills & Co......	6	4	20
,,	31	,, Bills Receivable	,,	8	12	,,	,,	,, W.G.Taylor.	7	10	00
,,	,,	,, Profit&Loss.	L.F 10	12	18						
				24	20					24	20

Dr.   R E N T A N D C H A R G E S.   Cr.

1868.			J.F.	$	c.	1868.			L.F	$	c.
Jan.	25	To Cash	6	30	00	Jan.	31	By Profit & Loss.	10	79	70
,,	29	,, do.	,,	49	70						
				79	70					79	70

I

Sixth Set—Ledger.

FOL. 10

Dr.   CASH.   Cr.

FOL. 10

1868.			L.F	$	c.	1868.			L.F	$	c.
Jan.	17	To am't brought forward....	4	1116	21	Jan.	17	By am't brought forward....	4	233	80
			J.F.						J.F.		
,,	,,	,, Morrison, T. & Co......	4	80	00	,,	19	,, Bills Payable	5	145	05
,,	23	,, Sundries....	5	496	50	,,	21	,, Warehouses and Stores.	,,	60	00
,,	30	,, J. Boyd & Co.	6	88	00	,,	25	,, Glynn, Mills & Co......	,,	800	00
,,	31	,, Bills Receivable	,,	848	88	,,	,,	,, Rent & ch'gs	6	30	00
,,	,,	,, do. do. ...	7	140	00	,,	29	,, do.	,,	49	70
						,,	,,	,, Profit & Loss.	,,	3	05
						,,	31	,, Glynn, Mills & Co......	,,	835	80
						,,	,,	,, Balance.....	8	612	19
				2769	59					2769	59
Feb.	1	To Balance....		612	19						

Dr.   PROFIT AND LOSS.   Cr.

1868.			J.F.	$	c.	1868.			L.F	$	c.
Jan.	29	To Cash......		3	05	Jan.	31	By Copperas...	1	9	40
			L.F			,,	,,	,, Opium.....	2	13	42½
,,	31	,, Alum......	1	1	00	,,	,,	,, Galls.......	2	2	80
,,	,,	,, Tobacco....	1	39	60	,,	,,	,, Clover Seed.	2	12	00
,,	,,	,, Sugar......	2	6	75	,,	,,	,, Barrel Staves	3	296	40
,,	,,	,, Rent & ch'rgs	9	79	70	,,	,,	,, Bottles.....	,,	5	10
,,	,,	,, Stock	1	844	69½	,,	,,	,, Wine.....	,,	178	50
						,,	,,	,, Salt........	6	96	03
						,,	,,	,, Herrings...	7	38	00
						,,	,,	,, Whisky . ..	,,	14	20
						,,	,,	,, Brandy,....	8	166	90
						,,	,,	,, Ashes......	9	129	80
						,,	,,	,, Discount....	,,	12	18
				974	79½					974	79½

Sixth Set—Ledger.

FOL. 11 DR.			BALANCE.				CR. FOL. 11	
1868.			J.F	$ c.	1868.		J.F	$ c.
Jan. 31	To Sundries, merchandise accounts ..		8	14809 95½	Jan. 31	By Personal Accounts	8	1548 00
,,	,,	,, Bills Receivble........	,,	352 00	,,	,, ,, Bills Payable	,,	8674 45
,,	,,	,, Warehouses & Stores ..	,,	4860 00	,,	,, ,, Stock	L.F 1	13769 49½
,,	,,	,, Cash	,,	612 19				
,,	,,	,, Personal accounts	,,	3357 80				
				23991 94½				23991 94½

DAY-BOOK—SEVENTH SET.

SECOND METHOD, COLLECTED FORM. (See note, page 88.)

TORONTO, 1st JANUARY, 1868.

J.F	INVENTORY OF PROPERTY.	*P.W.B.		$	c.
		70			
1	Goods on hand,—			$	c.
,,	Alum...... 7cwt. 3qrs. 0lbs., @ $2 80	21	70		
,,	Copperas .. 23 ,, 0 ,, 0 ,, ,, 1 15	26	45		
,,	Tobacco .. 12 ,, 1 ,, 13 ,, ,, 1 15 ℔ lb	1485	60		
,,	Sugar ... 12 ,, 3 ,, 0 ,, ,, 9 00 ,, ct.	114	75		
,,	Opium .... 73 ,, ,, 2 45 ,, lb	178	85		
,,	Galls...... 146 ,, ,, 50 ,, ,,	73	00		
,,	Cloverseed.. 12 ,, 2 ,, 0 ,, ,, 16 00 ,, ct.	200	00		
,,	Corkwood .... 8tons 5cwt., ,, 104 00 ,, tn	858	00		
,,	Barrel Staves .. 26 M., ,, 48 60 ,, M	1263	60		
,,	Bottles........ 8¼ gross, ,, 5 40 ,, gr	45	90		
,,	Wine .... 8 pipes, ,, 288 00 ,, p.	2304	00		
,,	Do. .... 4 ,, ,, 320 00 ,, ,,	1280	00		
,,	Do. .... 36 doz., ,, 9 60 ,, dz	345	60		
,,	Do. .... 73 ,, ,, 9 00 ,, ,,	657	00		
,,	Do. .... 109 ,, Cape, ,, 4 20 ,, ,,	457	80		
,,	Do. .... 3 ps. Teneriffe, ,, 192 00 ,, p.	576	00		
,,	Do. .... 4 ,, Lisbon, ,, 232 00 ,, ,,	928	00		
,,	Do. .... 5 butts Sherry, ,, 252 00 ,, bt	1260	00		
				†12076	25
1	Debts due to me,—				
,,	Reford & Dillon, Wellington Street..........	169	00		
,,	Chas. Moore & Co., do.	290	00		
				459	00
,,	Warehouse and Store, valued at			4800	00
				17335	25

* P. W. B. (Page Waste Book.)

† N.B.—We now charge the whole amount, $12076.25, to the general account of Merchandise, and not to each of the Accounts as in the former method, viz., Alum, Copperas, etc., etc.

W. R. ORR.

Sixth Set—Collectedly.

TORONTO, 1st JANUARY, 1868.

J.F.		P.W.B.	$	C.
1	Debts due by me,—	70		
,,	John Boyd & Co., Front St............. $409.30	,,		
,,	Morrison, Taylor & Co., Front St. 229.85	,,		
,,	Glynn, Mills & Co., London, Eng. 151.80	,,	790	95

———————— 1 ————————

| 3 | Received from Antonia Silva & Co., St. Ubes, Invoice of Salt, shipped per the Active, 33 tons, at $20 per ton...................................... | 71 ,, ,, | 660 | 00 |

———————— 2 ————————

| 3 | Bought of George Michie & Co., Front St., for 3 months' Bill, 70 barrels Lochfine Herrings, at $4 per bbl................................... | 71 ,, ,, | 280 | 00 |

———————— 3 ————————

| 3 | Bought of W. G. Taylor, London, England, 31 days, 4 cases Leghorn Hats, per list..................... Freight and Charges paid by him................. Commission for purchasing, 2 per cent............ | 71 ,, ,, ,, | 2940 139 58 3138 | 00 20 80 00 |

———————— 4 ————————

| 3 | Bought of Smith & Arthurs, Wellington St.,— 3 puncheons of Irish Whisky, Nos. 1 to 3, 168 gals., at $1.10 per gal .... Storage charged thereon............ .... | 71 ,, ,, ,, | 184 4 189 | 80 20 00 |

———————— 6 ————————

| 4 | Sold by F. G. Perkins & Co., Front St.,— 1 Pun. Irish Whisky, 56 gals., at $1.85 per gal. .... | 72 ,, | 103 | 60 |

———————— 6 ————————

| 4 | Sold Hugh Miller, King St.,— 1 Case Opium, 16½ lbs., at $2.90 per lb........... | 72 ,, | 47 | 85 |

Book-keeping—Seventh Set.

TORONTO, 7TH JANUARY, 1868.

J.F.		P.W.B.	$	C.
3	Received from Reford & Dillon, Wellington St.,— 4 Casks of Brandy, at $266......................	72 ,,	1064	00
	——————— 9 ———————			
4	Sold Smith & Arthurs, Wellington St.,— 1 Pun. Irish Whisky, 56 gals., at $1.90............	73 ,,	106	40
	——————— 11 ———————			
4	Sold Morrison, Taylor & Co., Front St.,— 6 M Barrel Staves, at $60 per M..................	73 ,,	360	00
	——————— 12 ———————			
4	Sold J. E. Smith & Co., Church St.,— 2 Pipes Port Wine, at $336.00 each............... 19 Doz. Cape do. ,, 4.60 doz................ 19 Do. btls. under ,, 50 do............. 8½ gross Empty bottles, at $6.00 gross...........	74 ,, ,, ,, ,,	672 87 9 51 ——— 819	00 40 50 00 ——— 90
	——————— 13 ———————			
3	Bought of Chas. Moore & Co., Wellington St., at 4 months,— 75 bbls. Pot Ashes, per invoice, at $18.60..........	74 ,,	1395	00
	——————— 13 ———————			
4	Sold John Boyd & Co., Front St., at 2½ per cent. for cash,— 14½ cwt. Copperas, at $1.30 per cwt.............	74 ,,	18	85
	John Boyd & Co. did not pay Cash for the Copperas, as was their intention at the time of purchase, therefore they are charged with the whole amount; if they had paid Cash, the 2½ per cent. would have been entered and deducted. W. R. ORR.			
	——————— 15 ———————			
4	Handed George Michie & Co., Front St.,— Delacour's acceptance, $200.....................	75 ,,	200	00
	——————— 17 ———————			
4	Sold Morrison, Taylor & Co., Front St., at 61 days, 12 tons St. Ubes Salt, at $25 per ton.............	75 ,,	300	00

Sixth Set—Collectedly.
TORONTO, 17TH JANUARY, 1868.

J.F.		P.W.B	$	C.
4	Sold John Boyd & Co., Front St., at 2½ per cent. for Cash,—	75		
	5 cwt. Alum, at $ 2.60 per cwt.	,,	13	00
	10 M Staves, ,, 60.00 ,, M..............	,,	600	00
	3 cwt. Clover Seed, at 20.00 ,, cwt............	,,	60	00
			673	00

——————————— 17 ———————————

4	Discount allowed Morrison, Taylor & Co., Front St., for 2 months' Interest......................	76 ,,	3	00

——————————— 23 ———————————

4	Sold Morrison, Taylor & Co., Front St., for 3 months' Bill,—	77		
	12 bbls. Pot Ashes, at $ 7.00 per bbl.............	,,	84	00
	15 do. Herrings, ,, 5.20 ,, do.	,,	78	00
	10 M Staves, ,, 60.00 ,, M.............	,,	600	00
	10 tons Salt, ,, 25.00 ,, ton.............	,,	250	00
			1012	00

——————————— 24 ———————————

4	Sold J. E. Smith & Co., Church St,—	77		
	1 cask French Brandy, $350.90.................	,,	350	90
	1 hhd. Sugar, 1200 lbs., at 9 c. per lb............	,,	108	00
	3 pipes Port Wine, at $340.00 per pipe	,,	1020	00
	30 doz. Cape do. ,, 4.30 ,, doz.	,,	129	00
			1607	90

——————————— 25 ———————————

4	Drawn on J. E. Smith & Co., Church St., in favor of Reford & Dillon, Wellington St., at 31 days, $1128, Discount allowed by Reford & Dillon for prompt payment............................ 10	78 ,,	1138	00

——————————— 29 ———————————

3	Received Invoice from Reford & Dillon, Wellington St., of Pearl Ashes shipped from Goderich, per Grand Trunk, 100 bbls., at $17.50 per bbl.........	79	1750	00

——————————— 21 ———————————

4	Sold to John Boyd & Co., Front St,— 50 bbls. Pearl Ashes, now on their way from Goderich, deliverable 3 days after arrival, at $20 per bbl...	79	1000	00

Book-keeping—Seventh Set.
TORONTO, 30TH JANUARY, 1868.

J.F.		P.W.B	$	C.
4	Discount allowed John Boyd & Co., Front St., for interest on Cash.................................	80 ,,		90
	——————— 31 ———————			
4	Error in charging Morrison, Taylor & Co., Front St., Pot Ashes, 12 bbls., at $7, instead of $19, say $12 per bbl...	82 ,, ,,	144	00
	——————— 31 ———————			
5	Drawn on J. E. Smith & Co., Church St., in favor of W. G. Taylor, London, England, at 31 days, for.....................................$1128.00 Discount allowed for prompt payment...... 10.00	82 ,, ,, ,,	1138	00
	——————— 31 ———————			
5	Error discovered in placing to the account of Smith & Arthurs, Wellington St., 1 pun. Irish Whisky, sold to F. & G. Perkins & Co., Front St., on Jan. 9th...	82 ,, ,,	106	40
	——————— 31 ———————			
5	Error in giving Credit to Morrison, Taylor & Co., Front St., for Cash, paid by John Boyd & Co., Front St., on Jan. 17th.....................	83 ,, ,,	80	00

Sixth Set—Collectedly.
TORONTO, 31ST JANUARY, 1868.

J.F					P.W.B.	$	C.
5	Inventory of Goods on hand,—				83		
		cwt. qrs. lbs.					
	Alum	2 3 0	@ $	2 80 ℔ cwt.	$ 7 70		
	Tobacco	12 0 5	,,	1 20 ,, lb.	1446 00		
	Opium	16½	,,	2 45 ,, ,,	40 42½		
	Galls	84	,,	50 ,, ,,	42 00		
	Cloverseed	9 2 0	,,	16 00 ,, cwt.	152 00		
	Corkwood......	8 tons 5 cwt.	,,	104 00 ,, ton.	858 00		
	Wine	6 pipes port	,,	288 00 ,, pipe	1728 00		
	Do.	1 ,,	,, ,,	320 00 ,, ,,	320 00		
	Do.	73 doz. ,,	,,	9 00 ,, doz.	657 00		
	Do.	36 ,,	,, ,,	9 60 ,, ,,	345 60		
	Do.	57 ,,	,, ,,	4 20 ,, ,,	239 40		
	Do.	3 ps. Teneriffe,		192 00 ,, pipe	576 00		
	Do.	4 ,, Lisbon,		232 00 ,, ,,	928 00		
	Do	5 bts Sherry,		252 00 ,, butt	1260 00		
	Salt...........	11 tons,	@	20 63 ,, ton.	226 93		
	Herrings	35 bbls.,	,,	4 00 ,, bbl.	140 00		
	Leghorn Hats..	4 cases,	,,	791 52 ,, case	3166 10		
	Irish Whiskey..	56 gals.,	,,	1 75 ,, gal.	98 00		
	Brandy	2 casks,	,,	266 00 each.	532 00		
	Ashes.........	63 bbls.,	,,	18 60 ℔ bbl.	1171 80		
	Do.	50 ,,	,,	17 50 ,, ,,	875 00		
						14809	95¾
					P.W.B.		
5	Cash on hand				84	612	19
	Bills Receivable on hand,—						
	Finlay & Co.'s acceptance			$	40 00		
	James Wilson's do.				62 00		
	Thos. Hodgen's do.				150 00		
	E. Carpenter's do.				100 00		
						352	00
5	Warehouse and Stores, valued at					4860	00
	Carried forward					20634	14¼

Book-keeping—Seventh Set.

(Sixth Set—Collectedly.)

TORONTO, 31st JANUARY, 1868.

J.F		P.W.B.	$	C.
	Brought forward		23634	14¼
5	List of Debts due to me,—	84		
	John Boyd & Co., Front Street ....$ 401 65			
	Morrison, Taylor & Co., Front Street.... 1286 15			
	Glynn, Mills & Co., London, Eng. 1488 20			
	F. & G. Perkins & Co., Front Street 10 00			
	J. E. Smith & Co., Church Street 171 80			
			3357	80
			23991	94¼
	————————31————————			
5	List of Debts due by me,—	85		
	Reford & Dillon, Wellington Street ......$ 443 00			
	Chas. Moore & Co., do. 1105 00			
			1548	00
5	List of Bills Payable,—	85		
	My note to N. Low $4000 00			
	,, acceptance to McDonnell & Co. 688 65			
	,, do. ,, Wm. Murray 72 80			
	,, do. ,, A. Silva & Co. 660 00			
	,, do. ,, Reford & Dillon. 1064 00			
	,, do. ,, Smith & Arthurs 189 00			
	,, do. ,, W. G. Taylor 2000 00			
			8674	45
			10222	45

Cash Book—Seventh Set.

FOL. I.   DR.   CASH.

1868.	J. F.			P. W. B.	$	C.
Jan.	1	1	To Stock amount on hand.................	69	*650	00
,,	7	2	,, Merchandise Sold E. Grant............	72	15	00
,,	9	2	,, F. & G. Perkins & Co., on ccount......	73	200	00
,,	11	2	,, Hugh Miller.........................	74	7	85
,,	16	2	,, Merchandise	75	100	00
,,	,,	,,	,, do.	,,	6	36
,,	17	,,	,, Morrison, Taylor & Co.................	76	137	00
,,	,,	,,	,, Morrison, Taylor & Co.................	,,	80	00
,,	23	,,	,, Merchandise sold Lyman, Elliott & Co...	.77	496	50
,,	30	2	,, John Boyd & Co., on account...........	80	88	00
,,	,,	,,	,, Bills Receivable (4 bills discounted)......	,,	857	00
,,	31	,,	,, Discount...........................	81	4	20
,,	,,	2	,, Bills Receivable, J. Wilson's acceptance..	,,	140	00
					†2781	91
Feb.	1		To Balance on hand.....................		612	19

* NOTE.—This amount, $650, is not now to be taken into the Journal, as it was journalized when the books were opened, 1st Jan. Balances, whether on the Debit or Credit side of the Cash-book, are never journalized, as the balance at the Debit was not received during the current month, nor was the Balance at the Credit paid out.

† NOTE.—The totals of the Cash by this mode are $12.32 greater than the totals of the Cash Account in the Ledger, by the former method (See Ledger, page 108), in consequence of the Bills Receivable discounted being entered in full on the Dr. side, and the Discount of these Bills on the Cr. ; but the Cash balance is the same. In the former set the net proceeds, only, of the Bills, appeared in the Cash account.

W. R. ORR.

Sixth Set—Collectedly.

CONTRA.   CR.   FOL. I.

1868.		J.F			P.W.B.	$	C.
Jan.	4	2	By Merchandise, paid duty and charges....		71	34	95
,,	7	,,	,, do. do.	....	73	69	85
,,	10	,,	,, do. do.	....	,,	20	90
,,	,,	,,	,, do. freight and do.	....	,,	28	10
,,	15	,,	,, George Michie & Co		75	80	00
,,	19	,,	,, Bills Payable, my accept. to Johnston & Co		76	145	05
,,	21	,,	,, Warehouse and Stores, paid S. Booth ..		77	60	00
,,	25	,,	,, Glynn, Mills & Co. (purchased draft)....		78	800	00
,,	,,	,,	,, Rent and Charges (paid rent of Warehouse		79	30	00
,,	29	,,	,, do. (Postage, Wages, etc.).		,,	49	70
,,	,,	3	,, Profit and Loss, deficient in settling		,,	3	05
,,	30	,,	,, Discount (for Interest 4 Bills discounted).		80	8	12
,,	,,	2	,, Glynn, Mills & Co. (purchased draft)		81	840	00
,,	31		,, Balance			612	19
						2781	91

Bills Receivable, January, 1868.

J. F.	No	When Received	From whom Received	By whom drawn, and place.	On whom drawn, and where.	Dates	To whom payable.	Time.	Due.	Sum.		How disposed of.
										$	c.	
,,	,,	,,	Stock	,,	J. Wilson	,,	Myself	,,	Jan. 23.	140	00	Rec'd payment
,,	,,	,,	do.	,,	E. & J. Kelly	,,	,,	,,	Feb 15.	225	60	Discounted.
,,	,,	,,	do.	,,	J. Harding	,,	,,	,,	Mar. 4..	71	40	do.
,,	,,	,,	do.	,,	S. Delacour	,,	,,	,,	,, 17..	200	00	G. Michie & Co
1										*637	00	
3	1	Jan. 11.	H. Miller	Finlay & Co.	Finlay & Co	,,	Myself	61 d'ys	,, 12..	40	00	
3	2	,, 17.	Morrison&Co	J. Tottenham	J. Tottenham	,,	,,	,,	Feb. 4..	160	00	Discounted.
,,	3	,, 30.	J. Boyd & Co.	J. Wilson	J. Wilson	,,	,,	,,	Mar. 4..	62	00	
,,	4	,,	do.	Kelly & Sons	Kelly & Sons	,,	,,	,,	April 3.	400	00	Discounted.
,,	5	,,	do.	T. Hodgens.	T. Hodgrens.	,,	,,	,,	,, 11..	150	00	
,,	6	,,	do.	E. Carpenter	E. Carpenter	,,	,,	,,	,, 20..	100	00	
										912	00	

* These Bills are in my possession and must be placed to my Credit, under the title of Stock, and to the debit of Bills Receivable. The amount, $637, must be journalized and posted before you commence the regular Month's Business.

Bills Payable, January, 1868.

J. F.	No	By whom drawn, and place.		Date.	To whom payable.	Time.	Accepted	Due.	Sum.		To whom paid, and when.	By whom paid.
									$	c.		
"	"	Stock	Toronto	"	N. Low	1 day	Jan. 1	Jan. 2	4000	00	Johnston 19 inst	Myself.
"	"	do.	do.	"	Johnston & Co.	19 do.	"	" 19	145	05		
"	"	do.	do.	"	McDonnell & Co	64 do.	"	Mar. 4	688	65		
"	"	do.	do.	"	Wm. Murray	103 do.	"	April 13	72	80		
									*4906	50		
1	1	A. Silva & Co.	St Ubes	Dec. 20	A. Silva & Co.	4 months	Jan. 7	April 23	660	00		
3	2	Reford & Dillon	Toronto	Jan. 14	Reford & Dillon	90 days	" 14	" 10	1064	00		
"	3	Smith &Arthurs	do.	"	Smith & Arthurs	2 months	" 14	" 16	189	00		
"	4	Myself	do.	Jan. 19	W. G. Taylor	31 days	" 19	Feb. 19	2000	00		
									3913	00		

* These Bills being due by me when I re-commence business, must be carried to the debit of Stock and to the Credit of Bills Payable. This amount of $4000.50 must be journalized and posted before commencing the regular business of the month.

SEVENTH SET.

JOURNALIZING SIXTH SET, COLLECTEDLY.*

REAL ACCOUNTS,

CASH AND MERCHANDISE, ALSO OF TRANSACTIONS BY BILLS, WITH DISCOUNT, INTEREST, &c., &c.

* See note, page 88.

Journal—Seventh Set. 123

(Sixth Set—Collectedly.)

FOL. I

TORONTO, 31st JANUARY, 1868.

	L.F			Page.	$	c.	$	c.
		1	Sundries Dr. to Stock,—					
Jan.	1	1	Cash as per..............C. B.	118			650	00
,,	,,	,,	Bills Receivable as per..B.R.B.	120			637	00
,,	,,	,,	Merchandise as per.......D.B.	110			12076	25
,,	,,	2	Reford & Dillon, Wellington Street, as per........D.B.	,,	169	00		
,,	,,	,,	Chas. Moore & Co., Wellington Street, as per........D.B.	,,	290	00		
							459	00
,,	,,	2	Warehouse & Store as per D.B.				4800	00
							18622	25
Jan.	1	1	Stock Dr. to Sundries,—				4906	50
,,	,,	2	Bills Payable as per,....B.P.B.	121				
,,	,,	3	John Boyd & Co., Front Street, as per..............D.B.	111	409	30		
,,	,,	,,	Morrison, Taylor & Co., Front Street, as per........D.B.	,,	229	85		
,,	,,	,,	Glynn, Mills & Co., London, England, as per......D.B.	,,	151	80		
							790	95
							5697	45

NOTE.—Proceed now to open accounts for the above in the Ledger, when this is done you have performed what is called opening the books.

The transactions of the month will then be journalized in the collected form from each book in use, viz. :—Cash Book, Bill Book and Day Book; the dates being in the first, and Ledger folio in the second column, at the left hand side of the Journal.

W. R. ORR.

* C. B. (Cash Book.) B. R. B. (Bills Receivable Book.) B. P. B. (Bills Payable Book.) D. B. (Day Book.)

Journal—Seventh Set.

FOL. 2

TORONTO, 31ST JANUARY, 1868.

	L.F			Page.	$	c.	$	c.
		1	Cash Dr. to Sundries ...C.B.	118				
Jan.	7	,,	Merchandise	,,	15	00		
,,	16	,,	do.	,,	100	00		
,,	,,	,,	do.	,,	6	36		
,,	23	,,	do.	,,	496	50		
							617	86
,,	9	3	F. G. Perkins & Co., Front Street	,,	200	00		
,,	11	4	Hugh Miller, King Street....	,,	7	85		
,,	17	3	Morrison, Taylor & Co., Front Street	,,	137	00		
,,	,,	,,	Morrison, Taylor & Co., Front Street	,,	80	00		
							217	00
,,	30	3	John Boyd & Co., Front Street	,,			88	00
,,	,,	1	Bills Receivable	,,	857	00		
,,	31	,,	do.	,,	140	00		
							997	00
,,	,,	4	Discount	,,			4	20
							2131	91

		1	Sundries Dr. to Cash ...C.B.	119				
Jan.	4	,,	Merchandise.................	,,	34	95		
,,	7	,,	do.	,,	69	85		
,,	10	,,	do.	,,	49	00		
							153	80
,,	15	4	George Michie & Co., Front Street	,,	80	00		
,,	19	2	Bills Payable.................	,,	145	05		
,,	21	,,	Warehouse and Stores.	,,	60	00		
,,	25	3	Glynn, Mills & Co., London, England	,,	800	00		
,,	30	,,	Glynn, Mills & Co., London, England	,,	840	00		
							1640	00
,,	25	4	Rent & Charges	,,	30	00		
,,	29	,,	do. do.	,,	49	70		
							79	70
			Carried forward to page 125..				2158	55

Sixth Set—Collectedly Journalized. 125

FOL. 3

TORONTO, 31ST JANUARY, 1868.

	L.F			Page.	$	C.	$	C.
			Sundries Dr. to Cash ...C.B.	119				
			Brought forward from page 124				2158	55
Jan	29	5	Profit and Loss	,,			3	05
,,	30	4	Discount	,,			8	12
							2169	72
		1	Bills Rec'ble Dr. to Sundries.					
Jan	11	4	Hugh Miller, King-st. No. 1 due 12th March..........B.R.B.	120			40	00
,,	17	3	Morrison, Taylor & Co., Front Street, No. 2	,,			160	00
,,	30	,,	John Boyd & Co., Front-st. No. 3, due 4th March	,,	62	00		
,,	,,	,,	John Boyd & Co., Front-st. No. 4, due 3rd April...........	,,	400	00		
,,	,,	,,	John Boyd & Co., Front-st. No. 5, due 11th April	,,	150	00		
,,	,,	,,	John Boyd & Co., Front-st. No. 6, due 20th April	,,	100	00		
							712	00
							912	00
		2	Sundries Dr. to Bills Payable.					
Jan	1	5	A. Silva & Co., St. Ubes, No. 1, due April 23rd ......B.P.B.	121	660	00		
,,	14	2	Reford & Dillon, Wellington-st. No. 2, due April 10th	,,	1064	00		
,,	,,	5	Smith & Arthurs, Wellington-st. No. 3, due April 16th	,,	189	00		
,,	19	5	W. G. Taylor, London, England, No. 4, due Feb. 19th........	,,	2000	00		
							3913	00
		1	Merchandise Dr. to Sundries.	P.D.B 111			660	00
Jan	1	5	A. Silva & Co., St. Ubes	,,			280	00
,,	2	4	George Michie & Co., Front-st.	,,			3138	00
,,	3	5	W. G. Taylor, London, England.	,,			189	00
,,	4	5	Smith & Arthurs, Wellington-st.	,,				
,,	7	2	Reford & Dillon, Wellington-st.	112	1064	00		
,,	29	,,	Do. do. do.	113	1750	00		
							2814	00
,,	13	,,	Chas. Moore & Co., do.	112			1395	00
							8476	00

Journal—Seventh Set.

FOL. 4

TORONTO, 31ST JANUARY, 1868.

	L.F			P.D.B	$	C.	$	C.
		1	Sundries Dr. to Merchandise	111				
Jan	6	3	F. & G. Perkins & Co., Front-st	,,			103	60
,,	6	4	Hugh Miller, King Street......	,,			47	85
,,	9	5	Smith & Arthurs, Wellington-st	112			106	40
,,	11	3	Morrison, Taylor & Co. Front-st	,,	360	00		
,,	17	,,	Morrison, Taylor & Co. ,,	,,	300	00		
,,	23	,,	Morrison, Taylor & Co. ,,	113	1012	00		
,,	31	,,	Morrison, Taylor & Co. ,,	114	144	00		
							1816	00
,,	12	6	J. E. Smith & Co., Church-st..	112	819	90		
,,	24	,,	J. E. Smith & Co., ,,	113	1607	90		
							2427	80
,,	13	3	John Boyd & Co., Front-st....	112	18	85		
,,	17	,,	John Boyd & Co., Front-st....	113	673	00		
,,	29	,,	John Boyd & Co., Front-st....	114	1000	00		
							1691	85
							6193	50
,,	15	4	George Michie & Co., Front Street, Dr.	112				
		1	To Bills Receivable............	,,			200	00
Jan	17	4	Discount Dr. to Sundries,—	113				
,,	,,	3	Morrison, Taylor & Co. Front-st	,,	3	00		
,,	30	3	John Boyd & Co., Front-st....	114		90		
							3	90
Jan	31	4	Sundries Dr. to Discount,—					
,,	25	2	Reford & Dillon, Wellington-st	113	10	00		
,,	31	5	W. G. Taylor, London, Eng..	114	10	00		
							20	00
,,	25	2	Reford & Dillon, Wellington Street, Dr.,—	113				
,,	,,	6	To J. E. Smith & Co., Church-st.				1128	00

Sixth Set—Collectedly Journalized.

TORONTO, 31ST JANUARY, 1868.

FOL. 5

Date		L.F	Description	P.D.B	$	C.	$	C.
		5	W. G. Taylor, London, Eng. Dr.,—					
Jan	31	6	To J. E. Smith & Co., Church-st.	114			1128	00
,,	,,	3	F. G. Perkins & Co., Front Street, Dr.—	114				
,,	,,	5	To Smith & Arthurs, Wellington Street	,,			106	40
,,	,,	3	Morrison, Taylor & Co. Front Street, Dr.—	114				
,,	,,	3	To John Boyd & Co., Front-st..	,,			80	00
		6	Balance Dr. to Sundries,—	115				
,,	,,	1	Cash	,,			612	19
,,	,,	1	Bills Receivable	,,			352	00
,,	,,	1	Merchandise	,,			14809	95¼
,,	,,	2	Warehouse and Stores	,,			4860	00
,,	,,	3	John Boyd & Co., Front-st....	116	401	65		
,,	,,	3	Morrison, Taylor & Co., Front-st	,,	1286	15		
,,	,,	3	Glynn, Mills & Co. London, Eng.	,,	1488	20		
,,	,,	3	F. G. Perkins & Co., Front-st..	,,	10	00		
,,	,,	6	J. E. Smith & Co., Church-st..	,,	171	80		
							3357	80
							23991	94½
		6	Sundries Dr. to Balance,—	116				
,,	,,	2	Reford & Dillon, Wellington-st.	,,	443	00		
,,	,,	2	Chas. Moore & Co., ,,	,,	1105	00		
							1548	00
,,	,,	2	Bills Payable.................	,,			8674	45
							10222	45

INDEX TO LEDGER.

SEVENTH SET.

(Sixth Set—Collected Form.)

B	L.F.	P	L.F.
Bills Receivable	1	Perkins, F. & G. & Co., Front St	3
Bills Payable	2	Profit & Loss	5
Boyd, John & Co., Front Street..	3		
Balance	6	**R**	
		Reford & Dillon, Wellington St..	2
C		Rent and Charges	4
Cash	1		
		S	
D		Stock	1
Discount	4	Silva, A. & Co., St. Ubes	5
G		Smith & Arthurs, Wellington St.	5
Glynn, Mills & Co., London,.. E	3	Smith, J. E. & Co., Church St ..	6
M		**T**	
Merchandise	1		
Moore, Chas. & Co., Wellington St	2	Taylor, W. G., London, England	5
Morrison, Taylor & Co., Front St	3		
Miller, H., King Street	4	**W**	
Michie, G. & Co., Front Street..	4	Warehouse and Stores	2

Ledger—Seventh Set.

FOL. 1

DR.   STOCK.   CR. FOL. 1

1868.			J.F.	$	c.	1868.			J.F.	$	c.
Jan.	1	To Sundries..	1	5697	45	Jan.	1	By Sundries..	1	18622	25
,,	31	,, Balance ..	L.F 6	13769	49½	,,	31	,, Profit & Loss	L.F 5	844	69¼
				19466	94¼					19466	94¼
						Feb.	1	By Balance ..		13769	49½

DR.   CASH.   CR.

1868.			J.F.	$	c.	1868.			J.F	$	c.
Jan.	1	To Stock......	1	650	00	Jan.	31	By Sundries...	3	2169	72
,,	31	,, Sundries...	2	2131	91	,,	,,	,, Balance....	L.F 6	612	19
				2781	91					2781	91
Feb.	1	To Balance....		612	19						

DR.   BILLS RECEIVABLE.   CR.

1868.			J.F	$	c.	1868.			J.F	$	c.
Jan.	1	To Stock	1	637	00	Jan.	31	By Cash......	2	997	00
,,	31	,, Sundries ..	3	912	00	,,	,,	,, G. Michie & Co.....	4	200	00
						,,	,,	,, Balance....	L.F 6	352	00
				1549	00					1549	00
Feb.	1	To Balance ..		352	00						

DR.   MERCHANDISE.   CR.

1868.			J.F	$	c.	1868			J.F	$	c.
Jan.	1	To Stock	1	12076	25	Jan.	31	By Cash......	2	617	86
,,	31	,, Cash......	2	153	80	,,	,,	,, Sundries	4	6193	50
,,	,,	,, Sundries ..	3	8476	00	,,	,,	,, Balance ..	L.F 6	14809	95¼
,,	,,	,, Profit & Loss.	L.F 5	915	26½						
				21621	31¼					21621	31¼
Feb.	1	To Balance ..		14809	95½						

Ledger—Seventh Set.

FOL. 2

Dr.　　REFORD & DILLON, Wellington-St.　　Cr.

1868.			J.F	$	c.	1868.			J.F	$	c.
Jan.	1	To Stock	1	169	00	Jan.	31	By Merchandise	3	2814	00
,,	31	,, B. Payable.	3	1064	00						
,,	,,	,, J. E. Smith & Co....	4	1128	00						
,,	,,	,, Discount ..	,,	10	00						
,,	,,	,, Balance ..	L.F 6	443	00						
				2814	00					2814	00
						Feb.	1	By Balance....		443	00

Dr.　　CHAS. MOORE & Co., Wellington-St.　　Cr.

1868.			J.F	$	c.	1868.			J.F	$	c.
Jan.	1	To Stock	1	290	00	Jan.	31	By Merchandise	3	1395	00
,,	31	,, Balance ..	L.F 6	1105	00						
				1395	00					1395	00
						Feb.	1	By Balance····		1105	00

Dr.　　WAREHOUSE & STORES.　　Cr.

1868.			J.F	$	c.	1868.			L.F	$	c.
Jan.	1	To Stock	1	4800	00	Jan.	31	By Balance ..	6	4860	00
,,	31	,, Cash......	2	60	00						
				4860	00					4860	00
Feb.	1	To Balance ..		4860	00						

Dr.　　BILLS PAYABLE.　　Cr.

1868.			J.F	$	c.	1868.			J.F	$	c.
Jan.	31	To Cash......	2	145	05	Jan.	1	By Stock	1	4906	50
,,	,,	,, Balance ..	L.F 6	8674	45	,,	21	,, Sundries ..	3	3913	00
				8819	50					8819	50
						Feb.	1	By Balance ..		8674	45

Sixth Set—Collectedly.

FOL. 3 — DR.   JOHN BOYD & Co., FRONT-ST.   CR. — FOL. 3

1868.			J.F	$	C.	1868.			J.F	$	C.
Jan.	31	To Merchandise	4	1691	85	Jan.	1	By Stock	1	409	30
						,,	31	,, Cash	2	88	00
						,,	,,	,, B. Receivable	3	712	00
						,,	,,	,, Discount	4		90
						,,	,,	,, Morrison, T&Co	5	80	60
						,,	,,	,, Balance	L.F 6	401	65
				1691	85					1691	85
Feb.	1	To Balance		401	65						

DR.   MORRISON, TAYLOR & Co., FRONT-ST.   CR.

1868.			J.F	$	C.	1868.			J.F	$	C.
Jan.	31	To Merchandise	4	1816	00	Jan.	1	By Stock	1	229	85
,,	,,	,, J. Boyd & Co	5	80	00	,,	31	,, Cash	2	217	00
						,,	,,	,, B. Rec'able	3	160	00
						,,	,,	,, Discount	4	3	00
						,,	,,	,, Balance	L.F 6	1286	15
				1896	00					1896	00
Feb.	1	To Balance		1286	15						

DR.   GLYNN, MILLS & Co., LONDON, ENG.   CR.

1868.			J.F	$	C.	1868.			J.F	$	C.
Jan.	31	To Cash	2	1640	00	Jan.	1	By Stock	1	151	80
						,,	31	,, Balance	L.F 6	1488	20
				1640	00					1640	00
Feb.	1	To Balance		1488	20						

DR.   F. & G. PERKINS & CO., FRONT-ST.   CR.

1868.			J.F	$	C.	1868.			J.F	$	C.
Jan.	31	To Merchandise	4	103	60	Jan.	31	By Cash	2	200	00
,,	,,	,, Smith & Arthurs	5	106	40	,,	,,	,, Balance	L.F 6	10	00
				210	00					210	00
Feb.	1	To Balance		10	00						

Ledger—Seventh Set.

FOL. 4

DR.   HUGH MILLER, KING-ST.   CR.

FOL. 4

1868.			J.F	$	C.	1868.			J.F	$	C.
Jan.	31	To Merchandise	4	47	85	Jan.	31	By Cash	2	7	85
						,,	,,	,, B. Rec'able	3	40	00
				47	85					47	85

DR.   DISCOUNT.   CR.

1868.			J.F	$	C.	1868.			J.F	$	C.
Jan.	31	To Cash	3	8	12	Jan.	31	By Cash	2	4	20
,,	,,	,, Sundries	4	3	90	,,	,,	,, Sundries		20	00
,,	,,	,, Profit & Loss	L.F 5	12	18						
				24	20					24	20

DR.   GEORGE MICHIE & Co., FRONT-ST.   CR.

1868.			J.F	$	C.	1868.			J.F	$	C.
Jan.	31	To Cash	2	80	00	Jan.	31	By Merchandise	3	280	00
,,	,,	,, B. Rec'able	4	200	00						
				280	00					280	00

DR.   RENT AND CHARGES.   CR.

1868.			J.F	$		1868.			L.F	$	C.
Jan.	31	To Cash	2	79	70	Jan.	31	By Profit & Loss	5	79	70

Sixth Set—Collectedly.

FOL. 5

Dr.   PROFIT AND LOSS.   Cr.

FOL. 5

1868.			J.F	$	c.	1868.			J.F	$	c.
Jan.	31	To Cash......	3	3	05	Jan.	31	By Merchandise	1	915	26¼
,,	,,	,, Rent & Ch'gs	4	79	70	,,	,,	,, Discount ..	4	12	18
,,	,,	,, Stock......	L F 1	844	69½						
				927	44¾					927	44¾

Dr.   ANTONIA SILVA & Co., St. Ubes.   Cr.

1868.			J.F	$		1868.			J.F	$	c.
Jan.	31	To B. Payable.	3	660	00	Jan.	31	By Merchandise	3	660	00

Dr.   SMITH & ARTHURS, Wellington-St.   Cr.

1868.			J.F	$	c.	1868.			J.F	$	c.
Jan.	31	To B. Payable.	3	189	00	Jan.	31	By Merchandise	3	189	00
,,	,,	,, Merchandise	4	106	40	,,	,,	,, F. & G. Perkins & Co	5	106	40
				295	40					295	40

Dr.   W. G. TAYLOR, London, Eng.   Cr.

1868.			J.F	$	c.	1868.			J.F	$	c.
Jan.	31	To B. Payable.	3	2000	00	Jan.	31	By Merchandise	3	3138	00
,,	,,	,, J. E. Smith & Co....	5	1128	00						
,,	,,	,, Discount ..	4	10	00						
				3138	00					3138	00

Ledger—Seventh Set.

FOL. 6   DR.   J. E. SMITH & Co., CHURCH-ST.   CR.   FOL. 6

1868.			J.F	$	c.	1868.			J.F	$	c.
Jan.	31	To Merchandise	4	2427	80	Jan.	31	By Reford & Dillon ..	4	1128	00
						,,	,,	,, W.G.Taylor	5	1128	00
						,,	,,	,, Balance ..	L.F 6	171	80
				2427	80					2427	80
Feb.	1	,, Balance.....		171	80						

DR.   BALANCE.   CR.

1868.			L.F	$	c.	1868.			L.F	$	c.
Jan.	31	To Cash......	1	612	19	Jan.	31	By Reford & Dillon ..	2	443	00
,,	,,	,, B. Rec'able	,,	352	00	,,	,,	,, C. Moore & Co	,,	1105	00
,,	,,	,, Merchandise	,,	14809	95½	,,	,,	,, B. Payable..	,,	8674	45
,,	,,	,, Warehouse, etc......	2	4860	00	,,	,,	,, Stock......	1	13769	49½
,,	,,	,, J. Boyd & Co	3	401	65						
,,	,,	,, Morrison, T. & Co....	,,	1286	15						
,,	,,	,, Glynn, Mills & Co....	,,	1488	20						
,,	,,	,, F. & G. Perkins & Co	,,	10	00						
,,	,,	,, J. E. Smith & Co....	6	171	80						
				23991	94½					23991	94½

BOOK-KEEPING—EIGHTH SET. 135

EXAMPLES

OF SINGLE AND JOINT CONSIGNMENTS, ADVENTURES, FACTORSHIPS, PARTNERSHIPS, &c.

If I purchase a Ship, I open an account for the Ship, debit that account to Cash, for the purchase money or to whatever other description of property I have given for it, and credit the account by whatever I receive by the Ship, as freight, &c., and, also, if I sell it, by whatever I may receive for it. If the account is to be balanced while the ship remains in my possession, I must enter the Ship estimated at its present value, on the Cr. side of the account; and then the difference between the two sides will show the gain or loss which has arisen out of my purchase.

The same directions are applicable to houses, land, or other property, from which I may receive returns without parting with it. I must open a separate account for every particular item of such property; for example, every house, every farm, &c., which I purchase, or let separately, I debit such accounts to Cash, for all expenses laid out upon them, and credit them by all returns received from them. When I balance such accounts, I must, as in the case of Ships, enter on the Cr. side, the present value of the property, and the difference between the sides will show my loss or gain.

If I ship goods on an adventure, I open an account for the adventure, describing it in whatever way may render it most distinct, as, Consignment per the ——— (the name of the ship,) to ——— (the name of the place), Consignee, Mr. or Messrs. ——— (the name of the person or persons) : or simply, Consignment or Adventure, No. 1, No. 2, &c., the particulars being recorded in the Waste

Book, I debit this account with the goods shipped, or with Cash laid out in purchasing goods for the adventure, and with all Charges; and credit the account with all returns.

If the goods be all sold, the difference of sides will show the result of the adventure. If part of the goods be unsold, I must, in balancing, enter the value of them on the Cr. side of the account, as in the former case, such value being taken as it originally stood, and stated in an inner column of the account, and a percentage deducted therefrom, of the supposed deduction, if any, in the value, leaving the net account, or apparent real value, to be extended in the proper column, to show the true state of the account.

If I receive goods to be sold on behalf of an employer, for a commission, I open an account of Goods for the Account of ———— (the employer), this account is made Dr. for all charges, and Cr. by all receipts on account of the goods. If I sell goods thus consigned to me on credit, I make the purchaser Dr. to this account of goods; when the goods are all sold and the account is to be closed, by my remitting Cash or Bills, the account is made Dr. to the Cash or Bills remitted, and to Profit and Loss for my commission; or if I have an account open for commissions, the amount of the commission is placed to the credit of that account. If the account is to be balanced before the goods are all sold, or the proceeds remitted, I open a personal account for my employer, and credit him therein with what I may have received from the sale of his goods, and debit him with what I have expended on the goods, also with my commission on the amount sold, up to the time when the balance is struck and furnished to him.

The chief peculiarity of accounts of goods received to be sold on commission, is, that the value of the goods received is not entered on the Dr. side of the account in my Ledger, because they do not belong to me. I keep the account of them in a separate book, as still belonging to my employer, although entrusted to my care; but, having entered on the Cr. side of the account of such goods whatever Cash or other property I receive for them, I enter on the Dr. side, what I remit to my employer, together with charges and commission. If I do not remit to him Cash that I receive for his goods immediately, I credit his personal account with the amount of his goods sold by me, and debit it with my commission. If I advance any proportion of the value of the goods consigned to me, before they be sold, I open a personal account with my employer as before alluded to, debit that account with the money advanced to him, and credit it for whatever I sell, the difference will then show how much he owes me, or how much I owe him.

There are three cases of partnership. *First*, when I entrust goods to another person to trade with on my behalf and his own under certain stipulations. In this case, I state the terms of the co-partnery in the Waste Book, and open an account for it in the Ledger, designating it briefly and clearly. If I engage in several such co-partneries, I may describe them, Company No. 1, No. 2, &c. This account is debited to the Goods or Cash, which I contribute to the joint stock-in-trade, and credited by everything either of Goods or Cash, &c., that I receive from it. When the account is to be balanced, my Partner must ascertain the value of the goods remaining unsold, estimate the profit and loss in the ordinary way, calculate my share of either. If he pay me my share of gain, or I pay my share of loss, I debit the account for what I pay to Cash, or credit it by Cash for what I receive, as the case may be. The difference between the two sides in the Company Account will show the profit or loss, which must be entered accordingly. If my Partner do not pay me my share of gain, or I do not pay my share of loss, I Cr. the account, By Balance for my share of gain, or Dr. it, To Balance for my share of loss, after which, the account is to be closed like any Goods Account, by Profit and Loss

K

The *second* case of partnership is, when I am entrusted with property to trade with, on behalf of myself and others, on certain stipulated terms. I enter the terms in my Waste Book, and open an account for the Company as before; but in this case, I open also an account for the " Goods in Company," or accounts for the different kinds of goods in Company. I debit these accounts for whatever goods or cash I contribute to the Company's stock. I then make the Company's account Dr. for all the outlay I incurred by it, and make it Cr. by all that I received for it; if the outlay was for goods to be added to the Company's stock, I make the account of "Goods in Co." Dr. for the outlay; and, if I receive for the Company, Cash or Bills, I make my own accounts of Cash or Bills Receivable, Dr. to the Company's account. If I purchase goods on credit for the Company, I make the account of the Goods in Co. Dr. to the person from whom I purchase. If I sell on Cr., on behalf of the Company, I make the person to whom they were sold Dr. to the Goods in Company.

When I would settle with my partner, I find the gain or loss upon the "Goods in Company" Account in the usual way, and that gain or loss upon the Goods, I transfer to the Partnership Account, making that account Dr. to the "Goods in Company" Account, for loss, or Cr. by it for gain. The difference between the two sides of the Co-partnery Account will show the gain or loss upon the whole business of the Company.

I then calculate the shares of gain or loss for each Partner, according to the terms of the Partnership. If I pay my Partner his share then the Company Account is Dr. to Cash, for his share of gain, and to Profit and Loss for mine. If his share is not paid, then I open an account for him personally, and make the Company Account Dr. to his Personal Account for his share, and to Profit and Loss for mine. If loss was sustained, and he pay his share, then the Company Account is Cr. by Cash for his payment, and by Profit and Loss for my share of loss ; if he do not pay at the time, I open, as before, a Personal Account for him, and make him Dr. to the Company Account for his share of the loss, and Profit and Loss Dr. for my share.

The *third* case of partnership is when the several Partners take part in the management of the joint trade. In that case books are kept as for the trade of an individual. The Real Accounts, as Cash, Bills, &c., are the accounts of the Company ; the Personal Accounts are accounts of persons dealing with the Company; and the Fictitious Accounts show the gains or losses of the Company. Besides these accounts, an account is opened for each Partner, and each is made Dr. for whatever he receives from the Company, and Cr. for whatever he pays on its behalf. When a settlement is to be made the books are balanced as in ordinary cases. The gain or loss is ascertained also, by comparing the two sides of the Profit and Loss Account. Here, however, occurs a difference between books belonging to a Company, and books belonging to an individual. The gains or losses are not properly gains or losses of the Company, but of the individual Partners of the Company, to be distributed among them according to their respective shares. The balance of the Profit and Loss Account, therefore, is not carried to the Stock Account, but it is divided among the Partners, and carried to their personal accounts ; if gain, to their credit ; if loss, to their debit. The Stock Account, therefore, does not show, as in ordinary cases, the net profit made, or loss incurred, for the Stock of the Company receives no accession by profit made, or diminution by loss sustained, the profit going to the individual Partners, and placed to the credit of their Personal Accounts; and loss being also charged to the Partners, by being carried to the debit of their Personal Accounts.

Different methods are adopted by different Book-keepers in closing the Stock Account of the books of a Company. Perhaps the following is as simple and clear as any. Place as usual the gross value of the property of every kind, actually in possession of the Company, including the debts due to them, on the Cr. side of the Stock Account. If profit has been made, this inventory will of course include it, showing an overplus above the standing capital. The Balance of the Balance Sheet, brought to the Dr. side of the Stock Account will correspond with the standing capital, exclusive of gain; and to make the Dr. side equal, bring the sums placed to the Cr. side of the Partners' Account to the Dr. side of Stock. The profits made, will then appear as debts due upon the Stock, to the Partners of the Company; and losses will appear on the Cr. side of Stock, as debts due by the Partners to the Company.

If any transactions took place previous to the balance being made, between the Company and any of the Partners, such as, his receiving money before profits are ascertained, his account must be balanced among the other Personal Accounts, before ascertaining the loss or gain of the Company. But the profits or losses of that period, and first ascertained in the balance, are merely to be entered to the Partners Personal Accounts, to stand to their debit or credit for the ensuing year.

If any Partner wishes his share of gain to be added to his share of capital in the Company, and the company agree to it, then his share of gain, after being entered to his credit, must be entered also on the debit side of his account, "To Stock," and from thence being carried to the Cr. side of the Stock Account, makes the intended increase to the capital of the Company. If the partnership is at the same time to be dissolved, the Stock on hand must be sold or valued, the debts inwards collected, and outwards paid, and each Partner's share of the property paid to him, or of debts received from him. It however frequently happens that some one or more of the partners, or some other person or company takes the stock and debt of the Company at a valuation, and then becomes Dr. to each of the Partners, for his share of the property, as per valuation.

EIGHTH SET.

WASTE BOOK.

The following transactions are copied from Brewster's Encyclopædia. These have been chosen partly because they comprise in a narrow compass the chief difficulties of Book-keeping, and partly to show that the directions are applicable to business transactions generally.

TORONTO, 1st JANUARY, 1868.

AN INVENTORY OF MY EFFECTS AND DEBTS ACTIVE, TAKEN THIS DATE BY ME, A. B.

J.F		$	c.
1	I have in ready money.....................$ 8000 00		
,,	In the Royal Canadian Bank.........:....... 16000 00		
,,	My House and Furniture are worth 7200 00		
,,	7 pipes of Port Wine, A..................... 2240 00		
,,	Delivered 4 pipes into Co. 1, under the directions of James Higgins 1280 00		
,,	Taken 5 tons of Madder into Co. 2, with John Scott (Mark A) 1200 00		
	Due to me,—		
1	By Robert Runner 400 00		
,,	,, John King, our account of Exchange in Co. 3 .... 2000 00		
		38320	00

BOOK-KEEPING.

TORONTO, 2ND JANUARY, 1868.

J. F.		$	c.
1	Bought of Thos. Willan, for ready money, 3 tons of Madder, at $10.66⅔ per cwt., mark B.	640	00
	——————— 2 ———————		
1	Sold for ready money, 1 pipe of Port Wine ...	376	00
	This transaction and the last are for Cash, and must be entered accordingly.		
	——————— 2 ———————		
1	Bartered with James Reeves, 1 pipe of Port Wine, for 1½ tons of Madder, at $12 per cwt., M. C.	360	00
	When one kind of goods is bartered for another, make that which comes in Dr. to that which goes out.		
	——————— 2 ———————		
1	Lent James Walsh, to be repaid me in one month, with interest at 5 per cent.	400	00
	——————— 4 ———————		
1	Drawn on John King, of London, O. A. of Exchange, a Bill of $200 at usance, favor of James Quinn, or order, value received of do.. at 1¼ per cent. advance............	202	50

I have entered into a Partnership with John King, of London, by which I draw Bills on him, and sell them, receiving the advantage of the Exchange. I had $2000 in his hands, as appears by the inventory of my goods, and this transaction is drawing a Bill on him and obtaining 1¼ per cent. for it. I have an Account for this Partnership, under the title, John King,

EIGHTH SET.

TORONTO, 4TH JANUARY, 1868.

our account of Exchange, Co. 3, and I make Cash Dr. to that account for the whole sum received. O. A., in the entry, signifies our Account.

———— 4 ————

J. F.		$	C.
1	Drawn on John King, of London, O. A. of Exchange, a Bill of $1800, at usance, favor of James Williams, or order, value received of do., at 1 per cent. advance............ This is a transaction similar to the last, and to be entered in the same manner.	1818	00

———— 4 ————

| 2 | Received from James Higgins, the account of the sales of our Red Wine,—
 The total sales of 8 pipes.........$2880 00
 His commission of 2½ per cent.... 72 00
 ————
 The net proceeds.............. 2808 00
 My half is.................... 1404 00
 Which he paid me by a draft on the Royal Canadian Bank for that sum, and which I lodged there. | 1404 | 00 |

James Higgins and I contribute each 4 pipes of Port Wine to be sold, and the profits equally divided; but as he is to have the charge of selling them, he is to receive, beside his share of the profits, 2½ per cent. commission. The value of my share of the Wine as stated in the inventory, was $1280; he sells the whole for $2880, his commission is $72, the remainder is $2808, which is to be equally divided between us; my share is $1404, which he pays me by a draft on the Royal Canadian Bank. I have already an account opened for this Partnership, under the title, "Adventure in Co. 1," which was debited to Stock, for the Wine embarked in it.

BOOK-KEEPING.

TORONTO, 4TH FEBRUARY, 1868.

I now credit it, By the Royal Canadian Bank for the amount received on its account.

―――――――――― 5 ――――――――――

J. F.		$	C.
2	Received from the Royal Canadian Bank, the balance of the Interest Account, ending 24th Dec.	160	00

In Canada, the Bankers give interest for money lodged with them, and take interest for money advanced by them. In settling this account, the balance was in my favor, and the Royal Canadian Bank pays me $160 interest. Here I may, either, first make the Royal Canadian Bank Dr. to interest or to Profit and Loss for the interest due, and then make Cash Dr. to Royal Canadian Bank for the payment of it ; or I may at once make Cash Dr. to Profit and Loss for the interest paid me by the Royal Canadian Bank.

―――――――――― 6 ――――――――――

2	Sold for the account of Co. 2, to James Taylor, for an accepted Draft on the Royal Canadian Bank, the 10 tons of Madder, marked A.,—			
	1 ton, at $16 per cwt................$ 320 00			
	9 ,, ,, 14 ,, ... 2520 00			
		2840 00		
	My commission on the Sale, at 2½ per cent 71 00			
		2769 00		
	My half is 1384 50			
	John Scott's half is.................. 1384 50			
			2840	00
	Lodged the Draft on the Royal Canadian Bank, and paid John Scott by my Draft on the Royal Canadian Bank		1384	50

EIGHTH SET.
TORONTO, 6TH JANUARY, 1868.

By the inventory it appears that I contributed 5 tons of Madder to a partnership entered into with John Scott, he contributing an equal quantity; the whole being under my charge, for which I am to receive a Commission, besides an equal share of the profits. I have already opened an account for this Partnership, under the title of Co. 2, with John Scott. I sell the whole for a draft on the Royal Canadian Bank. As in the case of Co. 1, I first deduct my commission, then I pay John Scott his half by a Draft on the Royal Canadian Bank. Here, in the first place, I make the Royal Canadian Bank Dr. to Co. 2 for the whole amount of the Draft which I have received upon it. I then make Co. 2 Dr. to Commission, or Profit and Loss for my Commission; and to John Scott's Personal Account for his half of the net proceeds, which I owe him. And lastly, I make John Scott's Personal Account Dr. to Royal Canadian Bank, for the Draft which I paid him. Or opening no Personal Account for John Scott, I might have made Co. 2 Dr. to Commission, and to Royal Canadian Bank, for the Draft given to John Scott.

---11---

J. F.		$	C.
2	Remitted to John King, of London, for our account of Exchange, John Ker's Draft of $1200, at usance, on Coutts & Co., of London, which I purchased by my Draft on the Royal Canadian Bank..................	1188	00

This is money remitted to John King, to be drawn for, agreeably to the terms of the Partnership.

BOOK-KEEPING.

TORONTO, 11TH JANUARY, 1868.

I make Co. 3 Dr. to Royal Canadian Bank, for the Draft by which I purchased the Bill on Coutts & Co.

	12	$	C.
J. F.			
2	Shipped in the Lark, of Leith, Paul Henry, master, and consigned to William Kane, of Hull, to sell for my account, 4½ tons of Madder, at First Cost,— 3 tons, B............$640.00 1½ tons, C............ 360.00 Paid freight, &c............ 54.00	1054	00

This is a case of Consignment. I open an account for voyage to Hull, and make it Dr. to the Madder, and to Cash for the Expenses.

	13	$	C.
2	Sold William Ker, at 2 months,— 1 pipe of Port Wine................	348	00

	13	$	C.
3	Bottled for the use of the house, ½ pipe of the Port Wine........................ And used the remaining half to fill those that leaked	160	00

I make the account of Charges, or of House expenses Dr. to Port Wine, for the ½ pipe bottled. The other ½ pipe I enter on the Cr. side of the Port Wine Account, in the inner column, to account for diminution of quantity, but do not carry out the value of it into the money column, unless I keep an account of Leakage, which would not be necessary.

EIGHTH SET.

TORONTO, 13TH JANUARY, 1868.

J. F.		$	C.
3	Counterbalanced by the desire of John King of London, what I owe him, by the Invoice of Madder, received this date, against what he owes me, by our Account of Exchange. —The balance to be brought to his account.—The balance to be divided is......	32	50
	He shipped in the Fame, James Lawson, master, 5 tons of madder, at $12 per cwt.	1200	00

I had, on commencing, $2000 in the hands of John King, for the Account of Co. 3, to which I afterwards add a Bill of $1200, but which I purchase for $1188. I drew upon him for two sums, making together $2000. So that he has of mine, according to this statement, $1188; but I had made profit by the Bills which I drew on him, which was to be equally divided with him. To close this account he sends me Madder, to the value of $1200, and desires me to settle the account, and to give him credit for what balance may be over. Here, I first make Madder Dr. to Co. 3. I then make the same Co. 3 Dr. to John King's Personal Account, for his share of the profit; and to Profit and Loss, for my share of it, *i. e.*, $16.25 each.

─────────────── 25 ───────────────

| 3 | Robert Runner is dead, and Insolvent—what he owes me is lost................... | 400 | 00 |

This appears to be a total loss. I make Profit and Loss Dr. to Robert Runner for the whole. Should I afterwards receive

148 BOOK-KEEPING.

TORONTO, 25TH JANUARY, 1868.

any dividend from his Estate, I should make Cash Dr. to Profit and Loss for it.

J. F.	26	$	C.
3	Bought of James Henry, at the Auction Sales, at Six Months, with the condition of the abatement of 1 per cent. per month for ready money,—		
	5 pipes of Port Wine, at $300 per pipe......	1500	00
	This Wine was bought on credit, and the name of the Agent of the Sales was James Henry. Port Wine, therefore, is Dr. to James Henry.		
	26		
3	Bought of James Ker, on my note, payable at 2 months,—		
	4 tons of Madder, at $11 per cwt..........	880	00
	In return for this Madder, I gave my own Note or Bill payable at 2 months. I therefore say, Madder Dr. to Bills Payable.		
	27		
3	Discounted to James Henry, the Agent of the Sales, my debt for the 5 pipes Port Wine,—		
	The Discount is............$ 90.00		
	The Sum due.............. 1410.00		
	————	1500	00
	Paid by my Draft on the Royal Canadian Bank		

In purchasing the Port Wine on the 26th, at six months, the Agent agreed that if I choose to pay ready money, he would allow me one per cent. for every month. I act upon this agreement, and take the Discount, amounting to $90; the balance

EIGHTH SET.

TORONTO, 27TH JANUARY, 1868.

$1410, I pay by a Draft on the Royal Canadian Bank. Say, James Henry Dr. to Royal Canadian Bank, and to Discount, or to Profit or Loss for Discount.

———————————— 27 ————————————

J. F.		$	C.
3	Discounted to James Ker, my Note, payable in 2 months, at 6 per cent. per annum. The Discount is ....$ 8.72 The Sum paid.................. 871.28	880	00

I had given James Ker, for Madder, purchased on the 26th, my Note payable in two months. He wishes for ready money, which I agree to give upon his allowing me the Discount or Interest for two months. The discount is $8.72, and I pay the remainder in Cash. Bills Payable had already been made Cr. by Madder; I now, therefore, make Bills Payable Dr. to Cash, and to Discount, or to Profit and Loss for Discount.

———————————— 28 ————————————

3	Paid James Taylor, the award of the Examiners who viewed the hogshead of Madder, M. A., by draft on the Royal Canadian Bank,— My half is......................:$21.00 John Scott's is................ 21.00	42	00

In company with John Scott, Co. No. 2, I had sold Madder to James Taylor, (see entry Jan. 6,) one hogshead of which proved to be damaged. This being examined by competent persons, they awarded $42 as the amount of the damage. This I pay in Cash, charging one-half to John Scott. Cash is Cr. by Profit and Loss, for my share of loss, and by John Scott for his.

_____28_____

J. F. 4	Paid for the honor of William Kane, of Hull, his Draft of $200 on James Henry, protested yesterday for non-payment................$200.00 Charges of Protest.............. 2.00 Commission, ½ per cent........ 1.00	$	C.
		203	00

William Kane, of Hull, to whom I had sent Goods on consignment, neglects to provide for the payment of a Bill when it becomes due, and it is protested. But I believing in his solvency, pay the Bill, with the expenses of protest for him, charging him Commission. William Kane is Dr. to Cash, for Bills and Charges, and to Commission or Profit and Loss for Commission.

_____2nd February_____

4	Received from William Kane, of Hull, an account of the sales of 4½ tons of Madder, consigned to him the 12th current,—
	The total sales......................$1529.00
	His charges...................$ 2.30
	Commission and Insurance,
	   4 per cent..................... 61.20
	                                     63.50		

		1465	50

EIGHTH SET.

TORONTO, 2ND FEBRUARY, 1868.

J. F.		$	c.
	For which he has remitted me a Draft of Lane & Co., on King & Co., at 7 day's sight, for $1668.50, which includes my former demand of $203	1668	50

William Kane having sold my Goods consigned to him, sends me returns of the Sales, deducting charges and his commission, enclosing a Draft or Bill at 7 days, for the amount due to me on the consignment, and also for the Bill which I had paid. Bills Receivable, therefore, is Dr. to Voyage to Hull for the net proceeds of the Consignment, and to William Kane, for the amount of the Bill, which I had paid for him, with the Charges and Commission.

2

4	Received from James Walsh, $400 lent him, with interest.........................	401	66

2

4	Paid the Expenses of the House for the last month ....,............$200.00 Salaries .... 80.00 Petty Charges 14.00		
		294	

BOOK-KEEPING.

TORONTO, 4TH FEBRUARY, 1868.

J. F.		$	C.
4	Took Stock and found on hand as follows:		
,,	Cash	8455	36
,,	In Royal Canadian Bank	16261	50
,,	House, &c.	7200	00
,,	Wine, 8 pipes	2460	00
,,	Madder, 9 tons	2079	60
,,	Bills Receivable	1668	50
,,	John Scott, H. A.............$ 21.00		
,,	William Ker 384.00		
		405	00
		38529	96
	———— 4 ————		
4	Debts due to me,—		
,,	John King, of London	16	25

This set may be balanced from the Books without taking Stock, as the quantities of the goods received and sent out were regularly entered. In real business, however, the goods on hand should be compared with the balances of the quantities shown by the books.

The Ledger is to be posted from the Journal and balanced, as in former sets; taking care, in the case of co-partneries and commissions, to follow the directions given in the introduction to this Set.

Eighth Set—Questions.

QUESTIONS ON THE EIGHTH SET.

Of what transactions does this Set treat? If you purchased a Ship, how would you enter the transaction in your books? Suppose you received a certain sum for freight, how would you enter it? How, if you sold the Ship? If you should balance the account whilst you have the ship, how would you enter the ship? With what other description of property would you pursue the same plan? If you ship goods on an adventure, how would you proceed? Suppose part of the goods were unsold, how would you manage when balancing the books? If you receive goods to be sold on behalf of an employer, for a commission, how would you open an account? When you sold goods, how would you enter the receipts? How would you enter Cash or Bills remitted to your employer? How, your Commission? What is the chief peculiarity of accounts of goods received to be sold on commission? How many cases of partnership? What is the first? In what book would you state the terms of the co-partnery? In what book would you open an account for it? How would you debit this account? How credit it? What must be done when the accounts are to be balanced? If your partner paid you your share of gain, how would you enter it? How, if you paid your share of loss? How would you manage, if you neither received your share of gain nor paid your share of loss? How is the account to be closed? What is the second case of partnership? What other accounts would you open in this, besides those in the former case? When you contribute goods or cash to the Company's stock, how do you enter it? How, if you received Cash or Bills? How, if you purchased goods on credit for the Company? How, if you sell on credit? When you would settle

BOOK-KEEPING.

with your partner, upon what account would you find the gain or loss? To what account would you transfer this when found? On what side of the account is the gain to go? On what the loss? What will the difference of the two sides of the Co-partnery Account show? If you pay your Partner his share, how would you enter it? What would you do if his share is not paid? If your Partner pays his share of a loss sustained, how do you enter it? If he does not pay it at the time, how then? What is the third case of partnership? How are the books kept in this case? What do the Real Accounts show? What do the Personal Accounts show? What the Fictitious? What peculiar accounts are necessary? When is a Partner made Dr.? When Cr.? On which side of the Partner's Account is gain entered? On which loss? How is the gain or loss stated in the Stock Account? Why is gain not stated on the Cr. side of the Stock Account, as in ordinary cases? If a Partner choose to add his share of gain to the Capital, and the Company agree to receive it, how is that to appear in the Partner's Account? How is it to appear in the Stock Account? If the partnership is to be dissolved, what must be done with the Stock? What with the debts? Suppose that the Stock of the Company, or the debts due to it, were bought by an Individual or Company, in what relation would that Individual or Company stand to the Partners?

EIGHTH SET.

SINGLE AND JOINT CONSIGNMENT,
ADVENTURES, FACTORSHIPS,
PARTNERSHIPS, &c.

JOURNAL.

FOL.
1

TORONTO, 1ST JANUARY, 1868.

L.F		P.D.B	$	C.	$	C.
1	Sundries Dr. to Stock,—	141				
,,	Cash		8000	00		
,,	Royal Canadian Bank		16000	00		
,,	House and Furniture		7200	00		
2	Port Wine, 7 pipes (A)		2240	00		
	Adventure in Company 1 with James Higgins, 4 pipes		1280	00		
,,	Madder in Company 2 with John Scott, 5 tons		1200	00		
,,	Robert Runner		400	00		
3	John King, our account Exchange in Company 3		2000	00		
					38320	00
	——————— 2 ———————					
3	Madder Dr.,—	142				
1	To Cash, 3 tons				640	00
	——————— 2 ———————					
1	Cash Dr.,—	142				
2	To Port Wine, 1 pipe				376	00
	——————— 2 ———————					
3	Madder Dr.,—	142				
2	To Port Wine				360	00
	——————— 2 ———————					
3	James Walsh Dr.,—	142				
1	To Cash				400	00
	——————— 4 ———————					
1	Cash Dr.,—	142				
3	To John King, O. A. Exchange Co. 3..				202	50
	——————— 4 ———————					
1	Cash Dr.,—	142				
3	To John King, O. A. Exchange Co. 3..				1818	00

EIGHTH SET. 157

FOL. 2

TORONTO, 4TH JANUARY, 1868.

L.F		P.D.B	$	C.	$	C.
1	Royal Canadian Bank Dr.,—	143				
2	To Adventure Co. 1				1404	00
	——— 5 ———					
1	Royal Canadian Bank Dr.,—	144				
4	To Profit and Loss for Interest				160	00
	——— 5 ———					
1	Cash Dr.,—	144				
1	To Royal Canadian Bank				160	00
	——— 6 ———					
	Sundries Dr. to Sundries,—	144				
1	Royal Canadian Bank, Madder Co. 2 A		2840	00		
2	Madder Co. 2, John Scott's half		1384	50		
2	Madder Co. 2, Commission		71	00		
3	John Scott, draft on R. C. B.		1384	50		
					5680	00
2	To Madder Co. 2		2840	00		
3	,, John Scott, his half		1384	50		
4	,, Commission		71	00		
1	,, Royal Canadian Bank Draft					
	,, Favor John Scott		1384	50		
					5680	00
	——— 11 ———					
3	John King, O. A. Co. 3, Dr.,—	145				
1	To Royal Canadian Bank				1188	00
	——— 12 ———					
4	Voyage to Hull, Dr. to Sundries,—	146				
3	Madder, 4½ tons		1000	00		
1	Cash		54	00		
					1054	00
	——— 13 ———					
5	William Ker Dr.,—	146				
2	To Port Wine, 1 pipe				384	00

JOURNAL.

FoL. 3

TORONTO, 13TH JANUARY, 1868.

L. F		P.D.B	$	C.	$	C.
5	Charges Dr.,—	146				
2	To Port Wine, half pipe				160	00
	,, Leakage, remaining half					
	———— 13 ————					
	Sundries Dr. to Sundries,—	147				
3	Madder D		1200	00		
3	John King, O. A. Exchange, his half..		16	25		
3	Do. do. do. my half..		16	25		
					1232	50
3	To John King, O. A. Exchange	147	1200	00		
5	,, do. his pt. ac. gained		16	25		
4	,, Profit and Loss do.		·16	25		
					1232	50
	———— 25 ————					
4	Profit and Loss Dr.,—	147				
2	To Robert Runner ....,.....				400	00
	———— 26 ————					
2	Port Wine Dr.,—	148				
5	To James Henry....................				1500	00
	———— 26 ————					
3	Madder Dr.,—	148				
6	To Bills Payable....................				880	00
	———— 27 ————					
5	James Henry Dr. to Sundries,—	148				
1	Royal Canadian Bank ....:...		1410	00		
4	Profit and Loss for Discount..........		90	00		
					1500	00
	———— 27 ————					
6	Bills Payable Dr. to Sundries,—	149				
1	Cash		871	28		
4	Profit and Loss for Discount..........		8	72		
					880	00
	———— 28 ————					
1	Sundries Dr. to Cash,—	149				
4	Profit and Loss—my half		21	00		
3	John Scott, H. A. his do.		21	00		
					42	00

EIGHTH SET. 159

FOL. 4

TORONTO, 28TH JANUARY, 1868.

L. F		P. D. B	$	C.	$	C.
6	William Kane Dr. to Sundries,—	150				
1	Cash		202	00		
4	Commission		1	00		
					203	00
	———— 2nd Feb. ————					
6	Bills Receivable Dr. to Sundries,—	150				
4	Voyage to Hull		1465	50		
6	William Kane		203	00		
					1668	50
	———— 2 ————					
1	Cash Dr.,—	151				
3	To James Walsh				401	66
	———— 2 ————					
3	James Walsh Dr.,—	151				
4	To Profit and Loss				1	66
	———— 2 ————					
5	Charges Dr.,—	151				
1	To Cash				294	00
	———— 4 ————					
6	Balance Dr. to Sundries,—	152				
1	Cash				8455	36
1	Royal Canadian Bank				16261	50
1	House and Furniture				7200	00
2	Wine, 8 pipes				2460	00
3	Madder, 9 tons				2079	60
6	Bills Receivable				1668	50
3	John Scott, H. A.		21	00		
5	William Ker		384	00		
					405	00
					38529	96
	———— 4 ————					
6	Balance Cr.,—	152				
5	By John King, H. A				16	25

EIGHTH SET.

A
	L.F.
Adventure, Co. 1	2

B
Bills Payable	6
Bills Receivable	6
Balance	6

C
Cash	1
Commission	4
Charges	5

H
House and Furniture	1
Henry, James	5

K
King, John, O. A.	3
Ker, William	5
King, John, pt. account	5
Kane, William	6

M
Madder, Co. 2	2
Madder	3

P
Profit & Loss	4

R
Royal Canadian Bank	1
Runner, Robert	2

S
Stock	1
Scott, John, H. A.	3

V
Voyage to Hull	4

W
Wine	2
Walsh, James	3

Ledger—Eighth Set.

FOL. 1

DR.   STOCK.   **CR.**   FOL. 1

1868.			L.F	$	c.	1868.			J.F	$	c.
Feb.	4	To Balance ..	6	38513	63	Jan.	1	By Sundries...	1	38320	00
						Feb.	4	,, Profit & Loss	L.F 4	193	63
				38513	63					38513	63
						,,	5	,, Balance....		38513	63

DR.   CASH.   **CR.**

1868.			J.F	$	c.	1868.			J.F	$	c.
Jan.	1	To Stock	1	8000	00	Jan.	2	By Madder ..	1	640	00
,,	2	,, Wine	,,	376	00	,,	,,	,, Jas. Walsh.	1	400	00
,,	4	,, J.King,O.A	,,	202	50	,,	12	,, Voy. to Hull	2	54	00
,,	,,	,, J.King,O.A	,,	1818	00	,,	27	,, B. Payable..	3	871	28
,,	5	,, Rl. C. Bank	2	160	00	,,	28	,, Sundries ..	,,	42	00
Feb.	2	,, Jas. Walsh.	4	401	66	,,	,,	,, Wm. Kane.	4	202	00
						Feb.	2	,, Charges ..	,,	294	00
						,,	4	,, Balance ..	L.F 6	8454	88
				10958	16					10958	16
,,	5	To Balance ..		8454	88							

DR.   ROYAL CANADIAN BANK.   **CR.**

1868.			J.F	$	c.	1868.			J.F	$	c.
Jan.	1	To Stock	1	16000	00	Jan.	5	By Cash......	2	160	00
,,	4	,, Adventure, Co. 1....	2	1404	00	,,	6	,, John Scott.	,,	1384	50
						,,	11	,, J.King,O.A	,,	1188	00
,,	5	,, Profit & Loss	,,	160	00	,,	27	,, Jas. Henry .	3	1410	00
,,	6	,, Madder,Co.2	,,	2840	00	Feb.	4	,, Balance ..	L.F 6	16261	50
				20404	00					20404	00
Feb.	5	,, Balance.....		16261	00							

DR.   HOUSE AND FURNITURE.   **CR.**

1868.			J.F	$	c.	1868.			L.F	$	c.
Jan.	1	To Stock	1	7200	00	Feb.	4	By Balance ..	6	7200	00
Feb.	5	To Balance ..		7200	00							

Ledger—Eighth Set.

FOL. 2   FOL. 2

DR.   WINE.   CR.

1868.			J.F	$	C.	1868.			J.F	$	C.
Jan.	1	To Stock	1	2240	00	Jan.	2	By Cash	1	376	00
,,	26	,, Jas. Henry.	3	1500	00	,,	,,	,, Madder ..	,,	360	00
						,,	13	,, Wm. Ker..	2	384	00
						,,	,,	,, Charges ..	3	160	00
						Feb.	4	By Balance....	L.F 6	2460	00
				3740	00					3740	00
Feb.	5	,, Balance ..		2460	00						

DR.   ADVENTURE, Co., 1,   CR.
WITH JOHN HIGGINS.

1868.			J.F	$	C.	1868.			J.F	$	C.
Jan.	1	To Stock	1	1280	00	Jan.	4	By R. C. Bank	2	1404	00
Feb.	4	,, Profit & Loss	L.F 4	124	00						
				1404	00					1404	00

DR.   MADDER, IN Co. 2,   CR.
WITH JOHN SCOTT.

1868.			J.F	$	C.	1868			J.F	$	C.
Jan.	1	To Stock	1	1200	00	Jan.	6	By R. C. Bank	2	2840	00
,,	6	,, John Scott.	2	1384	50						
,,	,,	,, Commission	,,	71	00						
Feb.	4	,, Profit & Loss	L.F 4	184	50						
				2840	00					2840	00

DR.   ROBERT RUNNER.   CR.

1868.			J.F	$	C.	1868.			J.F	$	C.
Jan.	1	To Stock	1	400	00	Jan.	25	By Profit & Loss	3	400	00

Ledger—Eighth Set.

FOL. 3 Dr. JOHN KING, O. A. OF EXCHANGE IN Co. 3. Cr. **FOL. 3**

1868.			J.F.	$	c.	1868.			J.F.	$	c.
Jan.	1	To Stock......	1	2000	00	Jan.	4	By Cash	1	202	50
,,	11	,, R. C. Bank .	2	1188	00	,,	,,	,, do.	,,	1818	00
,,	24	,, J. King's p. a.	3	16	25	,,	24	,, Madder	3	1200	00
,,	,,	,, Profit & Loss	,,	16	25						
				3220	50					3220	50

Dr. M A D D E R . **Cr.**

1868.			J.F.	$	c.	1868.			J.F.	$	c.
Jan.	2	To Cash	1	640	00	Jan.	12	By voy'ge to Hull	2	1000	00
,,	,,	,, Wine	,,	360	00				L.F		
,,	24	,, J.King,O.A	3	1200	00	Feb.	4	,, Balance ...	6	2080	00
,,	26	,, Bills Pay'ble	,,	880	00						
				3080	00					3080	00
Feb.	5	To Balance....		2080	00						

Dr. J A M E S W A L S H . **Cr.**

1868.			J.F.	$	c.	1868.			J.F.	$	c.
Jan.	2	To Cash	1	400	00	Feb.	2	By Cash	4	401	66
Feb.	,,	,, Profit & Loss	4	1	66						
				401	66					401	66

Dr. J O H N S C O T T, H. A. **Cr.**

1868.			J.F.	$	c.	1868.			J.F.	$	c.
Jan.	6	To R. C. Bank.	2	1384	50	Jan.	6	By Madder Co. 2	2	1384	50
,,	28	,, Cash	3	21	00	Feb.	4	,, Balance	L.F 6	21	00
				1405	50					1405	50
Feb.	5	To Balance....		21	00						

Ledger—Eighth Set.

FOL. 4

DR.   PROFIT AND LOSS.   CR.   FOL. 4

1868.			J.F.	$	C.	1868.			J.F.	$	C.
Jan.	25	To Robt. Runner	3	400	00	Jan.	5	By R. C. Bank.	2	160	00
,,	28	,, Cash.......	,,	21	00	,,	24	,, J. King, O.A	3	16	25
Feb.	4	,, Charges....	5	454	00	,,	27	,, Jas. Henry..	,,	90	00
			L.F			,,	,,	,, Bills Pay'ble	,,	8	72
,,	,,	,, Stock......	1	193	63	Feb.	2	,, Jas. Walsh..	4	1	66
						,,	4	,, Adventure, Co. 1....	2	124	00
						,,	,,	,, Madder,Co.2	2	184	50
						,,	,,	,, Commission.	4	72	00
						,,	,,	,, Vo'ge to Hull	,,	411	50
				1068	63					1068	63

DR.   COMMISSION.   CR.

1868.			L.F	$	C.	1868.			J.F.	$	C.
Feb.	4	To Profit & Loss.	4	72	00	Jan.	6	By Madder, Co. 2.........	2	71	00
						,,	28	" Wm. Kane..	4	1	00
				72	00					72	00

DR.   VOYAGE TO HULL.   CR.

1868.			J.F.	$	C.	1868.			J.F.	$	C.
Jan.	12	To Sundries...	2	1054	00	Feb.	2	By B. Receivable	4	1465	50
			L.F								
Feb.	4	,, Profit & Loss	4	411	50						
				1465	50					1465	50

Ledger—Eighth Set.

FOL. 5

DR.   WILLIAM KER.   CR.   FOL. 5

1868.		J.F.	$	C.	1868.		L.F	$	C.
Jan.	13	To Port Wine.	2	384	00	Feb.	4	By Balance ..	6	384	00
Feb.	5	To Balance....		384	00					384	00

DR.   CHARGES.   CR.

1868.			J.F	$	C.	1868.			L.F	$	C.
Jan.	13	To Port Wine.	3	160	00	Feb.	4	By Profit & Loss	4	454	00
Feb.	2	,, Cash......	4	294	00						
				454	00					454	00

DR.   JOHN KING'S PT. ACCOUNT.   CR.

1868.			L.F	$	C.	1868.			J.F.	$	C.
Feb.	4	To Balance ..	6	16	25	Jan.	24	By J. King, O. A	3	16	25
						Feb.	5	,, Balance....		16	25

DR.   JAMES HENRY.   CR.

1868.			J.F	$	C.	1868.			J.F	$	C.
Jan.	27	To Sundries ..	3	1500	00	Jan.	26	By Port Wine.	3	1500	00

Ledger—Eighth Set.

FOL. 6   DR.   **BILLS PAYABLE.**   CR.   FOL. 6

1868.			J.F	$	C.	1868.			J.F	$	C.
Jan.	27	To Sundries ..	3	880	00	Jan.	26	By Madder	3	880	00

DR.   **WILLIAM KANE.**   CR.

1868.			J.F	$	C.	1868.			J.F	$	C.
Jan.	28	To Sundries ..	4	203	00	Feb.	2	By B. Rec'ble ..	4	203	00

DR.   **BILLS RECEIVABLE.**   CR.

1868.			J.F	$	C.	1868.			L.F	$	C.
Feb.	2	To Sundries...	4	1668	50	Feb.	4	By Balance····	6	1668	50
Feb.	5	To Balance ..		1668	50						

DR.   **BALANCE.**   CR.

1868.			L.F	$	C.	1868.			L.F	$	C.
Feb.	4	To Cash......	1	8454	88	Feb.	4	By John King.	5	16	25
,,	,,	,, R. C. Bank	,,	16261	50	,,	,,	,, Stock	1	38513	63
,,	,,	,, House, etc.	,,	7200	00						
,,	,,	,, Wine......	2	2460	00						
,,	,,	,, Madder....	,,	2080	00						
,,	,,	,, John Scott.	3	21	00						
,,	,,	,, Wm. Ker..	5	384	00						
,,	,,	,, B. Rec'able	6	1668	50						
				38529	88					38529	88

NINTH SET.

FIFTH SET DOUBLE ENTRY CHANGED TO SINGLE.

Day-Book—Ninth Set.

TORONTO, 1st JANUARY, 1868.

L.F.		* P.W.B.	$	C.
1	Cr. Stock,— Goods as per Inventory	55	4868	45

———————— 1 ————————

| 1 | Cr. John Black & Co.,—
 Goods as per invoice .... | 55 | 470 | 75 |

———————— 3 ————————

| 1 | Cr. James White,—
 Goods as per invoice .... | 55 | 300 | 65 |

———————— 4 ————————

| 2 | Dr. A. Macarthur,—
 1 Euclid ....$ 1 50
 1 Walker's Dictionary............ 2 10
 6 Spelling Books, at 15 c. 90
 50 Reading Books, at 40 c. .... 20 00 | 55 | 24 | 50 |

———————— 5 ————————

| 1 | Cr. James White,—
 Goods as per invoice .... | 56 | 11 | 20 |

———————— 6 ————————

| 1 | Cr. John Black & Co.,—
 Goods as per invoice .... | 56 | 213 | 60 |

———————— 6 ————————

| 2 | Dr. A. Macarthur,—
 24 Scripture Geography, at 10 c......$ 2 40
 100 Maculloch's Reading, at 60 c..... 60 00
 20 Dictionaries, at 50 c. .... 10 00 | 56 | 72 | 40 |

———————— 8 ————————

| 2 | Dr. A. Macarthur,—
 10 Thompson's Arithmetic, at 60 c.....$6 00
 12 ,, Geography, at 40 c..... 4 80 | 57 | 10 | 80 |

* P. W. B. (Page Waste Book.)

Fifth Set, by Single Entry.

TORONTO, 9TH JANUARY, 1868.

L.F.		P.W.B	$	C.
2	To Stock, and found in my possession,—	57		
	Cash...	,,	227	81
	Goods	,,	5594	50
	Debts due to me.............................	,,	27	70
			5850	01
	———————— 9 ————————			
2	Debts due by me............................	57	44	35

Cash-Book—Ninth Set.

FOL. 1

DR.   CASH.

1868.	L.F.		P.W.B.	$	C.
Jan. 1	1	To Stock...............................	55	1019	50
,,	,,	,, Goods, shop sales..............	,,	52	87
,,	2	2	,, Profit & Loss, the late Mr. Gordon's Legacy............	,,	74	50
,,	,,	,, Goods, shop sales.............	,,	54	85
,,	3	,, ,, ,, ...	,,	45	48
,,	4	,, ,, ,, ...	56	20	45
,,	5	,, ,, ,, ...	,,	61	50
,,	6	2	,, Profit & Loss, received for my bargain on a house......	57	80	00
,,	,,	,, Goods, shop sales.............	,,	31	64
,,	8	2	,, A. Macarthur, on account...	,,	80	00
,,	,,	,, Goods, shop sales.............	,,	48	87
				1569	66
,,	9	To Balance...........................		227	81

Fifth Set, by Single Entry.

CONTRA.   CR.

FOL. 1

1868.	L.F.			P.W.B.	$	C.
Jan.	2	1	By James White, on account......	55	80	00
,,	4	,,	,, James White, ,, ...	56	160	00
,,	,,	2	,, Expenses, Clerk's salary, ½ yr.	,,	150	00
,,	5	1	,, J. Black & Co., remitted on ac't	,,	400	00
,,	6	,,	,, James White, on account......	,,	71	85
,,	,,	2	,, Expenses, ½ year's rent of Warehouse	,,	200	00
,,	8	1	,, J. Black & Co., remitted on ac't	57	240	00
,,	9	2	,, Profit & Loss, money lost......	,,	40	00
,,	,,	,,	,, Balance........................		227	81
					1569	66

Ledger—Ninth Set.

Fol.. I   Fifth Set by Single Entry.   FOL. I

DR.   STOCK.   CR.

1868.			L.F	$	C.	1868.			P.D B.	$	C.
Jan.	9	To Profit & Loss, Expenses, &c.	2	235	50	Jan.	1	By Goods	168	4868	45
,,	,,	,, Balance, Net Capital......	,,*	5805	66	,,	,,	,, Cash......	170	1019	50
						,,	9	,, Gain on Goods...		153	21
				6041	16					6041	16
						Jan.	10	,, Balance ..		5805	66

DR.   JOHN BLACK & Co.   CR.

1868.			P.D B.	$	C.	1868.			P.D B.	$	C.
Jan.	5	To Cash ..C.B.	171	400	00	Jan.	1	By Goods	168	470	75
,,	8	,, do.	,,	240	00	,,	6	,, do.	,,	213	60
,,	9	,, Balance ..	L.F 2	44	35						
				684	35					684	35
						Jan.	10	By Balance....		44	35

DR.   JAMES WHITE.   CR.

1868.			P.D B.	$	C.	1868.			P.D B.	$	C.
Jan.	2	To Cash ..C.B.	171	80	00	Jan.	3	By Goods	168	300	65
,,	4	,, do.	,,	160	00	,,	5	,, do.	,,	11	20
,,	6	,, do.	,,	71	85						
				311	85					311	85

* It will be seen by comparing the above amount, $5305.66, that it agrees with the amount on hand as shown by the double entry method, Stock Account, page 63. The $235.50, on the debit side of stock, is my net loss for Expenses, etc. And the $153.21 is my net gain on goods sold.   W. R. ORR.

Ledger—Ninth Set.

Fifth Set by Single Entry.

FOL. 2   FOL. 2

DR.   A. MACARTHUR.   CR.

1868.			P.D B.	$	C.	1868.			P.D B.	$	C.
Jan.	4	To Goods	168	24	50	Jan.	8	By Cash..C.B.	170	80	00
,,	6	,, do.	,,	72	40				L F		
,,	8	,, do.	,,	10	80	,,	9	,, Balance ..	2	27	70
				107	70					107	70
Jan.	10	To Balance ..		27	70						

DR.   PROFIT AND LOSS.*   CR.

1868.			P.D B.	$	C.	1868.			P.D B.	$	C.
Jan.	9	To Cash..C.B.	171	40	00	Jan.	2	By Cash	170	74	50
,,	,,	,, Expenses ..	L.F 2	350	00	,,	8	,, do.	,,	80	00
						,,	9	,, Stock	L.F 1	235	50
				390	00					390	00

DR.   E X P E N S E S.*   CR.

1868.			P.D B.	$	C.	1868.			L.F	$	C.
Jan.	4	To Cash..C.B.	171	150	00	Jan.	9	By Profit & Loss	2	350	00
,,	6	,, do.	,,	200	00						
				350	00					350	00

DR.   BALANCE.   CR.

1868.			P.D B.	$	C.	1868.			L.F	$	C.
Jan.	9	To Cash	169	227	81	Jan.	9	By J. Black & Co......	1	44	35
,,	,,	,, Goods	169	5594	50	,,	,,	,, Stock	,,	5805	66
,,	,,	,, A. Macarthur	L.F 2	27	70						
				5850	01					5850	01

* I have not found in any treatise on Book-keeping—in which a "Single Entry" set is given—that the Nominal Accounts, such as Expenses, Profit and Loss, etc., have been kept.

Ledger—Ninth Set.

The reason, I suppose, is, the apparent difficulty in closing the books if such accounts were opened; but I think the satisfactory manner in which this set is closed, shows the difficulty to be only apparent. And it must be remembered that if these accounts are not kept, the expenses and casual gains and losses can not be shown at all. It is matter of astonishment that Morrison and Jackson, standard authors, should have overlooked this matter. Some of our American authors get over the difficulty by a subterfuge, viz., opening personal accounts. I think the subject of great importance, as I believe Single Entry better adapted to Retail business than Double Entry, as it does not require more than half the labor and expense, and is quite as satisfactory. Double Entry Book-keeping is valuable only to the trader when he can ascertain the exact amount of goods sold, which can not be practically done in a retail business

W. R. ORR.

BOOK-KEEPING.

SUBSIDIARY BOOKS.

When the transactions connected with any particular account in the Ledger are very numerous and small, it is usual to keep a record of them in a book by themselves, and to insert in the Ledger only the sums of the transactions added up at stated intervals.

For example, it would be obviously ridiculous to enter into the Ledger every shilling or sixpence paid out or received. An account of such small sums, therefore, is kept in a book by themselves, and added up once a week or once a month, and only the weekly or monthly sums put into the Ledger.

Larger cash transactions are often treated in the same way. All receipts and payments are entered on the Dr. and Cr. sides of a Cash Book, and the sum of each side brought once a month into the Ledger, by which contrivance there never can be more entries in the Ledger than *twelve* on each side, namely, *one* for each month in the year.

Sales are often managed in the same way. A book is kept for recording sales only, and the amount of sales added weekly or monthly to the Ledger. In some extensive retail trades every shopman is made to keep a book, which is added up every day, and the amount transferred to a general Sales Book, which again is added up once a week or month, and the sum entered in the Journal or Ledger. Sometimes, in such trades, only one Sales Book is kept in the shop, and every shopman writes every sale that he makes on a slip of paper, and hands it to the Book-keeper, who enters it in the Sales Book.

BOOK-KEEPING.

EXAMPLES OF A BOOK OF HOUSE EXPENSES.

1868.		House Expenses Dr. to Cash.	$	c.	$	c.
Jan.	1	For a Scrubbing Brush............		20		
,,	,,	,, mending a pair of Bellows...		10		
,,	,,	,, a new Tea Kettle............	1	50		
,,	,,	,, mending the Crane and 3 hooks........................	1	00		
,,	,,	,, a Fish.........................		50		
,,	6	,, 3 Washing Tubs...............	1	80		
,,	7	,, tinning a large pot and 4 saucepans		93		
					6	03
,,	9	,, a Goose and 2 Ducks......	1	20		
,,	10	,, a Turkey	1	20		
,,	11	,, the Baker's Bill.............	3	93		
,,	,,	,, ,, Butcher's Bill............	24	30		
,,	13	,, 3 lbs of Sausages............		30		
,,	14	,, a peck of Oysters............		60		
,,	16	,, a do. Onions............		10		
					31	63
,,	17	,, a new Fire-shovel and Tongs	1	70		
,,	,,	,, a large Stewpan..............	1	70		
,,	19	,, the Apothecary's Bill.........	14	00		
,,	20	,, a load of Hay...............	6	00		
,,	21	,, do. Straw	4	00		
,,	,,	,, the Farrier's shoeing White-foot		50		
,,	,,	,, curing Coachman's broken shin	4	20		
,,	,,	,, mending the Clock........	2	10		
					34	20
		Carried forward to page 177			71	86

SUBSIDIARY BOOKS. 177

1868.		House Expenses Dr. to Cash, (*Continued.*)	$	c.	$	c.
		Brought forward from page 176			71	86
Jan.	23	For a new Jack-line...............		40		
,,	24	,, the Cook's Bill...............	3	50		
,,	,,	,, a Turbot.......................	2	10		
,,	26	,, a dozen of large Eels......	1	50		
,,	27	,, a do. of Lemons..........		30		
,,	28	,, a Firkin of Butter...........	5	60		
,,	29	,, a Cheshire Cheese, 20 lbs., at 17 c........................	3	40		
,,	,,	,, the Baker's Bill...............	4	30		
,,	31	,, a Quarter's Rent...............	40	00		
					61	10
					132	86

These sums of each week's expenses, viz., $6.03, or 31.63, &c., are, at the end of each week, entered on the Cr. side of the Cash Book, "By house expenses," or by Profit and Loss for House Expenses.

NOTE.—This book will serve as an example for any description of Petty Cash Book.

W. R. ORR.

CASH BOOK.

The Cash Book is kept precisely on the same principles with the Cash Account in the Ledger; it is headed, on that account, Cash Dr., Contra Cr., the title, Cash, meaning myself in regard to Cash.

Whatever Cash is received, therefore, is entered on the Dr. side and whatever is paid out, is entered on the Cr. side.

BOOK-KEEPING.

EXAMPLE OF

1868.		Cash. Dr.	$	c.
Jan.	1	To Stock brought from the last month...	32396	84
,,	2	,, Sir Robt. Johnston, received in full...	120	00
,,	6	,, Ship James, received in full of John Herbert, for 1-16th..................	500	00
,,	8	,, Ship James, received of Capt. John Smith, in full for 1-16th.............	500	00
,,	17	,, Wm. Baker, Esq., received in part...	500	00
,,	20	,, Canary, for one pipe sold to William Dello	120	00
,,	25	,, Sundry accounts	696	00
			34832	84

1868.			$	c.
Feb.	1	To Balance brought from last month....	27957	74
,,	10	,, Ship James, received of William Evans in full for 1-16th............	500	00
,,	12	,, Ship James, received of James Jackson in full for 1-16th...............	500	00
,,	14	,, Ship James, received of Thomas Jones in full for 1-16th............	500	00
,,	20	,, John Hammond, Esq., rec'd in full...	400	00
,,	28	,, Wm. Warner, received in full.........	137	40
			29995	14

SUBSIDIARY BOOKS.

A CASH BOOK.

1868.		Contra. Cr.	$	c.
Jan.	4	By Ship James, paid in part...............	300	00
,,	9	,, James Allen, paid in full...............	5700	00
,,	23	,, Thos. Preston, Esq., paid in part......	357	40
,,	26	,, Ship James, paid Thos. Young for Joiner's Work...............................	83	40
,,	27	,, Ship James, paid T. Pierce in full for Rigging..	110	90
,,	28	,, Ship James, paid D. Smith in full for Repairs	161	60
,,	30	,, Ship James, paid Nathaniel Westal in full for Painting.....................	28	90
,,	31	,, House Expenses, paid Sundry Charges this month...........................	132	90
,,	,,	,, Balance remaining in hand.............	27957	74
			34832	84

1868.			$	c.
Feb.	3	By Ship James, paid the Block-maker in full	79	50
,,	7	,, Ship James, paid the Ship Chandler in full	2802	60
,,	14	,, Voyage to Amsterdam, consigned to Jacob Van Hoove.........................	561	57
,,	24	,, Voyage to Amsterdam, paid J. Adams for insuring 100 bags of Pepper	28	07
,,	27	,, Ship James, paid John Jones in full for Beef and Pork	438	10
,,	28	,, House Expenses, paid Sundry Charges this month...........................	159	37
,,	,,	,, Balance remaining in hand.............	25925	93
			29995	14

In transferring the entries of this book into the Ledger, the sum of each month only is entered at the end of the month. The sum of the Dr. side in the Cash Book is entered on the Dr. side in the Ledger, " To Sundries received this month ;" and the sum on the Cr. side of the Cash Book is entered on the Cr. side of the Ledger, " By Sundries paid this month." This abridgment, however, only affects the *Cash Account* in the Ledger; for every particular sum paid or received during the month must be entered to its corresponding account in the Ledger. Thus, after entering the sums of the month of January on the Dr. and Cr. sides respectively as above directed, I must turn to the account of Sir Robert Johnstone, Cr. side, and enter, " By Cash, $120." Then to the account of Ship James, Cr. side, and enter, " By Cash, $500." Having thus entered all the sums on the Dr. side, I must do precisely the same with the sums on the Cr. side. I must turn to the account of Ship James, Dr. side, and enter, " To Cash, $300." Then to the account of James Allen, Dr. side, and enter, " To Cash, $5700," and thus with all the other entries.

In the foregoing example of a Cash Book, the Cash is balanced every month, and the balance on hand carried to the following month. In entering the sums, therefore, in the Ledger, care must be taken to subtract these balances before making the entry. Thus, the entry in the Dr. side of the Cash Account in the Ledger for January is not $34832.84, but only $2436.

For April, it is not $29995.14, but deducting the balance, it is only $2037.40. So the Cr. side entries are transferred before the two sides are compared, and the balance entered.

BOOK OF CHARGES ON MERCHANDISE.

This is a subsidiary book in all respects like the book of House Expenses, and is treated in the same manner.

SUBSIDIARY BOOKS.

INVOICE BOOK, OUTWARD AND INWARD.

The Invoice Book Outward is used chiefly by factors or agents, and contains copies of Invoices of goods sent abroad.

The Invoice Book Inwards contains the Invoices of all goods received. This book is usually a common paper book, in which is pasted the original Invoices, with the charges added to them. Many book-keepers enter into the Journal from these books, other book-keepers prefer copying the Invoices into an Invoice book.

THE SALES BOOK.

In extensive retail trades, the Sales Book serves a purpose analogous to that of the Cash Book. It keeps the details of sales which are entered in the Ledger in sums at stated times, as once a week, or once a month. It is a book indispensable to factors or agents. It was formerly explained, that in accounts of goods received on consignments, the value of the goods is not entered, but merely the expenses, on them, the receipts, for them, and the returns made to the consigner. But the accounts of the quantity and the sales of the goods for each consignment, are kept in the *Sales Book*, and it is from this book that the consigner is furnished with an account of the goods with which he has entrusted his agent.

BOOKS OF BILLS RECEIVABLE AND BILLS PAYABLE.

These books contain in column, an account of every Bill received or paid away, stating the date, the drawer, the acceptor, the sum, the time due, &c.

BOOK-KEEPING.

THE LETTER BOOK.

This book contains copies of all letters sent out. These copies are now very generally taken by a copying machine. Letters inwards should be kept and arranged alphabetically, by the names of the writers, so that it is less necessary to keep copies of them.

POCKET BOOK.

When a Merchant transacts business from home, or when he attends markets, fairs, &c., he should keep a Pocket-book, in which to mark down every transaction, so that when he returns he may be able accurately to enter his transactions in the principal books.

GENERAL OBSERVATIONS.

The pupil who has carefully posted and balanced the foregoing Sets of Book-keeping transactions must have learned that the chief skill in this art lies in a judicious selection of accounts; for after the accounts are determined upon, the posting and balancing of them are mere matters of routine. Every diversity of trade or manufacture will necessarily have some modifications peculiar to itself; but a steady adherence to a few general principles, such as the following, will conduct a Book-keeper through the intricacies of any descrption of business transactions.

An account must be opened for every species of property or adventure, the gain or loss on which is to be computed separately; such as goods of every kind, ships, houses, voyages, partnerships, in short every form in which the merchant's property is embarked. When no advantage would be obtained by keeping a separate account of gain or loss, on different kinds of goods, they must be classed under one head as goods, merchandise, houses, &c. Every such account of property represents myself, or is my own account in regard to such property. Thus, when Cash or any kind of Goods is made Dr., it is I who am made Dr. When Cash is made Cr., it is I who am made Cr.

An account must be opened with every person or company with whom I have dealings on credit, on either side, for it is obvious that I cannot have a correct account of the state of my affairs unless I know what I owe, or what others owe to me.

Every kind of property that comes into my hands so as to become my own, must be entered on the Dr. side of the account of that kind of property; and every kind of property that passes out of my hands so as to cease to be mine, must be entered on the Cr. side of its own account. When property comes into my hands, but not so as to become my own, as when goods are consigned to me, I do not receive them into my Ledger, but keep an account of them in a separate book, merely entering in my Ledger what I pay out or receive on account of them.

If such goods become my own, I then open an account for them, or enter them to some account already open. When goods or any species of property goes out from me, still continuing to be mine, as when I send out goods on consignment, I do not enter it to the person's account to whom it is entrusted, but to the voyage, adventure, consignment, &c., to which it may be transferred.

Every description of outlay for which no kind of property is received in return, or of income, for which no kind of property is exchanged, the amount of which when the books are to be balanced it is requisite to know, must have an account opened for it, such as interest of money, borrowed or lent, discount of bills, rent, wages, house expenses, gifts, legacies, &c. But if the general account only of such outlays and incomes is required, they may be placed at once to the Dr. or Cr. of the Profit and Loss Account. If any of them be kept separately, the balance must be placed to the Dr. or Cr. of the Profit and Loss Account, as all such accounts of outlays or incomes are merely sub-divisions or branches of the Profit and Loss Account.

Every transaction must be entered on two accounts, the Dr. side of the one, and the Cr. side of the other; and consequently every sum posted in one account, must either be entered on the opposite side of another account, or divided among several other accounts.

This rule is so absolute and universal, that at any stage of the progress of keeping the books the sum of all the Cr. sides must be equal to the sum of all the Dr. sides. The ascertaining of this is called a trial balance, which may be made at any time.

Bills are treated like any other property, even Bills Payable; that is, my own engagement to pay money put into the form of a bill, and given out of my hands, are so treated, and accounts are opened for Bills Receivable or Bills Payable, on the same principles on which an account is opened for Cash, or any species of goods.

If a merchant, in balancing his books, would obtain a just view of the state of his affairs, he must not be satisfied with valuing his goods on hand at the price which they cost him, nor the debts due to him as if the amount of them were already in his hands in cash, but must make such deductions as the following:—

GENERAL OBSERVATIONS.

1. For deterioration of goods, by being kept, if any. This in any description of fancy goods must be considerable.

2. For the expense of collecting debts.

3. For the interest of money on debts not yet due, including Bills Receivable.

For the probable amount of bad debts.

These deductions should be placed on the Dr. side of the Profit and Loss account, so as to diminish the profits by so much.

ON CLOSING THE DIFFERENT KINDS OF ACCOUNTS.

1. All Personal Accounts are closed by the Balance Account.

2. All Real Accounts, except the Cash and Bills Receivable, are closed by a double balance.

First, the quantity of any kind of goods remaining on hand, or property remaining in any voyage, adventure, consignment, constitutes the balance of the account opened for that description of property.

It is therefore entered to the Cr. of the Account, By Balance.

Secondly, after this balance is entered, the difference between the sums of the Dr. and Cr. sides of the account is the gain or loss upon that account, and the account is to be closed by the Profit and Loss Account.

The Cash Account is closed by the Balance Account, because there is no such difference between the quantity of Cash remaining on hand, and the value of it, as there is between the quantity of any other kind of property, and its value in Cash.

All subordinate accounts of loss or gain, such as interest, Charges, &c., are closed by the Profit and Loss Account, being accounted but branches of that account.

The Profit and Loss Account and the Balance Account are closed by the Stock Account; and when the balances of these two accounts are added to the proper sides of the Stock Account, the two sides of that account will be equal, if the books have been correctly kept.

A SYNOPSIS OR COMPENDIUM OF MERCHANTS' ACCOUNTS.

Containing Particular Rules for the true stating of Debtor and Creditor, in all cases that can happen in the whole course of a Merchant's Dealing.

The Accounts of Merchants are of three sorts, viz. :—

I. Proper; wherein the Merchant trades by and for himself; which is either Domestic, *i. e.*, Inland and at Home; or Foreign, *i.e.*, Abroad.

II. Factorage; wherein the Merchant acts as Factor in Commission, for one that employs him; and this, also, is either Domestic or Foreign.

III. In Company; wherein two or more Merchants join together in trade, and have each a share of the gain, or bear a share of the loss, in proportion to his share in the Stock; as is taught in the rules of Fellowship.

1. OF PROPER ACCOUNTS.

I. DOMESTIC.

IN RECEIVING AND PAYING MONEY.

CASE 1.—When an inventory is taken of the Ready Money, Goods, Voyages, and Debts, belonging or owing to me;

RULE.—Dr. those several parcels and parties, Cr. Stock or Principal.

CASE 2.—When an inventory is taken of the Debts owing by me;

Compendium of Merchants' Accounts.

RULE.—Dr. Stock or Capital, Cr. the several parties to whom the same are due.

CASE 3.—When money is received of one man for the use of another, or for his own use;

RULE.—Dr. Cash, Cr. the person for whose use it is received. The same when money is received for goods formerly sold.

CASE 4.—When money is paid to one man for the use of another, or for his own use;

RULE.—Dr. the person for whose use it is paid, Cr. Cash. The same when money is paid for goods formerly bought.

CASE 5.—When money is lent;

RULE.—Dr. the borrower for the principal, Cr. Cash.

CASE 6.—When money is borrowed;

RULE.—Dr. Cash, Cr. the lender for the principal.

CASE 7.—When interest is received for money lent;

RULE.—Dr. Cash, Cr. Profit and Loss.

CASE 8.—When interest is become due to me, and booked before received;

RULE.—Dr. the person who owes it, Cr. Profit and Loss.

CASE 9.—When interest is paid for money borrowed;

RULE.—Dr. Profit and Loss, Cr. Cash.

CASE 10.—When interest is become due from me to another, and booked before paid;

RULE.—Dr. Profit and Loss, Cr. the person to whom it is due.

CASE 11.—When Charges are paid on Goods in my own possession;

RULE.—Dr. those goods, Cr. Cash.

CASE 12.—When Charges are paid on petty disbursements in trade;

RULE.—Dr. Charges on Merchandise, Cr. Cash.

CASE 13.—When Charges are paid on House-keeping and all expenses thereunto belonging;

RULE.—Dr. Profit and Loss or House expenses, Cr. Cash.

CASE 14.—When India Stock, Bank Stock, South Sea Stock, or Annuity is bought;

Compendium of Merchants' Accounts.

Rule.—Dr. such Stock or Annuity, Cr. Cash. The same there be a call of $20, &c., per cent. upon my share in any capital Stock.

Case 15.—When Interest is become due to me on such Stock or Annuity, and booked before received:

Rule.—Dr. the Stock or Annuity, Cr. Profit and Loss.

Case 16.—When India Stock, Bank Stock, South Sea Stock, or Annuity is sold;

Rule.—Dr. Cash, Cr. such Stock or Annuity.

Case 17.—When my debtor compounds with me, and I receive part of the debt for the whole;

Rule—Cr. the person who compounds for the whole debt, by Cash for what I receive, and by Profit and Loss for what I lose.

Case 18.—When I compound with my Creditor, and pay him part of the debt for the whole;

Rule.—Dr. the person who receives it, To Cash for what I pay, and to Profit and Loss for what is abated.

Case 19.—When a Legacy is bequeathed to me;

Rule.—Dr. the Executor, Cr. Profit and Loss.

Case 20.—When a Legacy is received;

Rule.—Dr. Cash, Cr. the Executor. If received before entered, Dr. Cash, Cr. Profit and Loss.

Case 21.—When I receive a Legacy for the use of another, myself being the Executor;

Rule.—Dr. Cash, Cr. the Legatee.

Case 22.—When I pay a Legacy for the use of another, myself being Executor.

Rule.—Dr. the Legatee, Cr. Cash.

Case 23.—When I receive money by assignment;

Rule.—Dr. Cash, Cr. the Assignor.

Case 24.—When I give an Assignment, or Order, or Bill on my debtor to my creditor;

Rule.—Dr. my Creditor, Cr. my Debtor.

Compendium of Merchants' Accounts.

CASE 25.—When I pay money to another by the Assignment or Order of my Creditor;
RULE.—Dr. my Creditor, Cr. Cash.

CASE 26.—When I receive a Promissory Note in payment, and book it;
RULE.—Dr. Bills Receivable, Cr. the person of whom you receive it in payment.

CASE 27.—When I deliver the said note in payment afterwards;
RULE.—Dr. the person who receives it, Cr. Bills Receivable.

CASE 28.—When I pay Charges on House-keeping, and all thereunto belonging;
RULE.—Dr. Profit and Loss, Cr. Cash.

IN BUYING AND SELLING GOODS.

CASE 29.—When I buy goods for present money;
RULE.—Dr. the goods bought, Cr. Cash.

CASE 30.—When I buy goods on trust;
RULE.—Dr. the Goods, Cr. the Seller. The same when payments are made to me, at several times, only mentioning in the Journal the several times of payment. The same, also, when goods are taken in lieu of a debt, either in part or in the whole.

CASE 31.—When I require an abatement on goods bought on trust, after they are booked, on the account of defects;
RULE.—Dr. the Seller for the abatement, Cr. the Goods bought. If the account of Goods be closed, Dr. the Seller, Cr. Profit and Loss.

CASE 32.—When I buy goods for part ready money, and part trust;
RULE.—Dr. the Goods, Cr. the Seller for the whole. Then Dr. the Seller for what I pay, Cr. Cash for the same sum. Or, Dr the Goods to Cash for what I pay, and to the Seller for what remains unpaid.

CASE 33.—When I buy goods for part ready money, part trust, and part bills;

Compendium of Merchants' Accounts.

Rule.—Dr. the Goods to Cash for what I pay, to Bills Receivable, and to the Seller for the rest.

Case 34.—When I sell goods for present money;
Rule.—Dr. Cash to the goods.

Case 35.—When I sell goods on trust; .
Rule. Dr. the Buyer to the goods. The same when payments are made to me, at several times, only mentioning in the Journal the several times of payment. The same, also, when goods are sold in lieu of a debt, either in part or in the whole.

Case 36.—When I make an abatement on goods sold on trust, after they are booked, on the account of defect;
Rule.—Dr. the goods for the abatement to the buyer. If the account of goods be closed, Dr. Profit and Loss to buyer.

Case 37.—When I sell goods for part ready money, and part on credit;
Rule.—Dr. the Buyer for the whole of the goods. Then Dr. Cash for what I receive to the buyer. Or, Dr. Sundries to the goods, Cash for the money received, the Buyer for what remains unpaid.

Case 38.—When I sell goods for part ready money, part trust, and part bills receivable;
Rule.—Cr. the Goods by cash for what is received, by bills receivable, and by the buyer for the rest.

Case 39.—When I buy several sorts of goods for ready money;
Rule.—Dr. each of them for its respective value to Cash.

Case 40.—When I buy several sorts of goods upon trust;
Rule.—Dr. each of them for its respective value, Cr. the Seller for the whole.

Case 41.—When I sell several sorts of goods for ready money;
Rule.—Dr. Cash to Sundries for the whole value, Cr. each sort for its respective sum.

Case 42.—When I sell several sorts of Goods on trust;
Rule.—Dr. the buyer to sundries for the whole value, Cr. each sort for its respective sum.

Compendium of Merchants' Accounts.

CASE 43.—When I want rebate to be made on the present payment of money, for goods bought upon credit;

RULE.—Dr. the Seller to Sundries for the whole sum, Cr. Cash for the sum paid, Cr. Profit and Loss for the rebate.

NOTE.—This is supposed to happen a day or two after the goods are bought and booked.

CASE 44.—When I make rebate on the present receiving of money for goods sold upon trust;

RULE.—Dr. Cash for the sum received, Dr. Profit and Loss for the sum rebated, Cr. the buyer by Sundries for the whole sum.

NOTE.—This is supposed to happen a day or two after the goods are sold and booked.

CASE 45.—When I buy goods of a debtor, for a debt due to me, their value amounting to more than the debt, and the overplus is paid back in money presently;

RULE.—Dr. the Goods to Sundries for the whole sum, Cr. the Seller for so much as his debt was, Cr. Cash for the overplus.

NOTE.—If several sorts of goods had been bought, and the overplus returned by me, then first Dr. each sort for its respective value; Cr. the Seller by Sundries for their whole value; secondly, Dr. the Seller for the overplus paid back, Cr. Cash for the same sum.

CASE 46.—When I sell goods to a creditor, for a debt due to him, their value amounting to more than the debt, and the overplus is returned to me in money presently;

RULE.—Dr. the Buyer for so much as was owing to him, Dr. Cash for the overplus received, Cr. the Goods sold by sundries for the whole sum.

NOTE.—If several sorts of goods had been sold, and the overplus returned to me then, first Dr. the Buyer to Sundries for their whole value, Cr. each sort for its respective value; secondly, Dr. Cash for so much as is received, and Cr. the Buyer for the same sum.

BARTER.

CASE 47.—When I give one sort of goods for another sort of equal value;

RULE.—Dr. the Goods received, Cr. the Goods delivered.

CASE 48.—When I give one sort of goods for another sort of greater or less value;

Compendium of Merchants' Accounts.

RULE.—First, Dr. the Person who receives my goods, Cr. those goods; secondly, Dr. the Goods received by me, Cr. the person who delivers them.

CASE 49.—When I give one sort of goods for several other sorts of equal value;

RULE.—Dr. each particular sort of goods received for its respective value, Cr. the Goods delivered by sundries for the whole value.

CASE 50.—When I give one sort of goods for several other sorts of greater or less value;

RULE.—First, Dr. each particular sort of goods received for its respective value, as above, Cr. the Seller by sundries for the whole; secondly, Dr. the same Person, as Buyer, and Cr. the Goods which he has bought.

CASE 51.—When I give several sorts of goods for one sort of equal value;

RULE.—Dr. the goods received to sundries for their value, Cr. each particular sort of goods delivered, for its respective value.

CASE 52.—When I give several sorts of goods for one sort of greater or less value;

RULE.—First, Dr. the Person to whom the Goods are delivered to sundries, for their whole value, Cr. those Goods severally for their respective sums; secondly, Dr. the goods received, Cr. the Seller.

CASE 53.—When I give several sorts of goods for several other sorts, either of equal, greater, or less value;

RULE.—First, Dr. each particular sort of Goods received for its respective value, Cr. the Seller of them by sundries for the whole value; secondly, Dr. the same Person as Buyer of the Goods delivered to him, to sundries for the whole value of them, Cr. each particular sort for its respective value.

CASE 54.—When I sell goods of one sort for part goods of another sort and part ready money;

RULE.—Dr. the Goods received for their value, Dr. Cash for the sum received, Cr. the goods sold by Sundries for their value.

Compendium of Merchants' Accounts.

CASE 55.—When I sell goods of one sort for part goods of another sort, part ready money, and part credit.

RULE.—Dr. Sundries, viz., the Goods received for their value, Cash for the sum received, the Seller for the rest; Cr. the goods sold by sundries for their value.

CASE 56.—When I sell goods ot one sort for part goods of another sort, part ready money, part trust, and part bills;

RULE.—Dr. Sundries, viz., the good received for their value, Cash for the sum received, the Seller for what he owes, and Bills Receivable; Cr. the goods sold by sundries for their value.

CASE 57.—When I buy goods of one sort, for part goods of another sort, and part ready money;

RULE.—Dr. the Goods bought to Sundries, Cr. the goods delivered for their value, Cr. Cash for the money paid.

CASE 58.—When I buy goods of one sort, for part goods of another sort, part ready money, and part credit or trust;

RULE.—Dr. the Goods bought to sundries, Cr. the Goods delivered for their value, Cr. Cash for the money paid, and Cr. the Seller for the rest.

CASE 59.—When I buy Goods of one sort, for part goods of another sort, part ready money, part trust, and part bills receivable;

RULE.—Dr. the Goods bought to sundries, Cr. the goods delivered for their value, Cr. Cash for the money paid, Cr. the Seller for what is due to him, and Cr. Bills Receivable for the amount of bill.

SHIPPING.

CASE 60.—When I buy a ship for ready money;
RULE.—Dr. the Ship, Cr. Cash.

NOTE.—The same for a ship fitted out, in which I have a share.

CASE 61.—When I buy a ship for part ready money and part trust;

RULE.—Dr. the Ship to sundries, Cr. Cash for the money paid, Cr. the Seller for the rest.

NOTE.—This is the same as Case 32, foregoing, which see.

CASE 62.—When I sell a Ship for ready money ;
RULE.—Dr. Cash, Cr. the Ship.

CASE 63.—When I sell a ship for part ready money and part trust ;
RULE.—Dr. Cash for the money received, Dr. the Buyer for what remains due, Cr. the Ship by sundries for the whole.

NOTE.—This is the same as Case 37, foregoing, which see.

FREIGHT.

CASE 64.—When I receive freight ;
RULE.—Dr. Cash, Cr. the Ship.

CASE 65.—When I pay freight ;
RULE.—Dr. the particular Voyage, Cr. Cash.

LEGACY.

CASE 66.—When I receive a legacy in houses, lands, or goods ;
RULE.—Dr. those Houses, Lands, or Goods, Cr. Profit and Loss.

BILLS.

CASE 67.—When I buy a bill of another for ready money, and receive discount ;
RULE.—Dr. Bills Receivable, Cr. Cash for the sum paid, Cr. Profit and Loss for the discount.

CASE 68.—When I sell a bill for ready money and give discount ;
RULE.—Dr. Cash for the sum received, Dr. Profit and Loss for the discount, Cr. Bills Receivable by sundries for the whole sum.

II. FOREIGN.

GOODS.

CASE 1.—When goods are sent to sea for my own account, which were formerly entered in my books ;

Compendium of Merchants' Accounts.

Rule.—Dr. Voyage to ——, Consigned to ——Cr. the Goods.

Case 2.—When goods are sent to sea for my own account, which were bought for present money, with all charges paid thereon;

Rule.—Dr. Voyage to ——, Consigned to ——, Cr. Cash.

Case 3.—When goods are sent to sea for my own account, which were bought on trust;

Rule.—Dr. Voyage to ——. Consigned to ——, Cr. the Seller.

Case 4.—When goods are sent to sea for my factor's account, which were formerly entered in my books;

Rule.—Dr. Factor's Account Current, Cr. the Goods.

Case 5.—When goods are sent to sea for my factor's account, which were bought for present money, with all charges paid thereon;

Rule.—Dr. the Factor's Account, Cr. Cash.

Case 6.—When goods are sent to sea for my factor's account, which were bought on trust;

Rule.—Dr. Factor's Account Current, Cr. the Seller.

PREMIUM OF INSURANCE.

Case 7.—When my goods are insured by another person, and I pay the premium presently;

Rule.—Dr. Voyage to ——, Consigned to ——, Cr. Cash.

Case 8.—When my goods are insured by another person, and I do not pay the premium presently;

Rule.—Dr. Voyage to ——, Consigned to ——, Cr. the Insurer.

Case 9.—When I pay the premium upon advice that my goods are safely arrived;

Rule.—Dr. the Insurer, Cr. Cash.

Case 10.—When the goods of another person are insured by me, and I receive the premium presently;

Rule.—Dr. Cash, Cr. Insurance.

Case 11.—When the goods of another person are insured by me, and I do not receive the premium presently;

Rule.—Dr. the Person whose goods I have insured, Cr. Insurance.

Case 12.—When I receive the premium afterwards;
Rule.—Dr. Cash, Cr. the Payer.

MONEY.

Case 13.—When I receive a premium with advance for the insurance of goods formerly sent to sea; *i. e.*, if I receive the premium in dollars, and sell them for more, and receive the sterling immediately;

Rule.—Dr. Cash to Sundries, Cr. the person who paid the dollars for what he paid them at, Cr. Profit and Loss for the gain in the payment.

Case 14.—When I sell them for gain, and receive the sterling some time afterwards;

Rule.—Dr. Cash for the gain only, Cr. Profit and Loss for the same sum.

Note.—The other part of this cash was entered in my books before.

Case 15.—When I sell the aforesaid dollars for more to my creditor;

Rule.—Dr. the Receiver to sundries, Cr. Cash for the value of the dollars as they were at first received, Cr. Profit and Loss for my gain in the payment.

Note.—If my creditor had received the said dollars immediately, the Remitter must be Cr. instead of Cash.

Case 16.—When I receive a premium with loss, for the insurance of goods formerly sent to sea; *i.e.*, if I receive the premium in dollars, and sell them for less, and receive the sterling immediately;

Rule.—Dr. Cash for what I sold them at, Dr. Profit and Loss for the loss, Cr. the Payer by sundries for what I at first received them at.

Case 17.—When I sell them for loss, and receive the sterling some time afterwards;

Compendium of Merchants' Accounts.

RULE.—Dr. Profit and Loss for the Loss only, Cr. Cash for the same sum.

NOTE.—The value of the dollars which I received them at was entered in my books before.

CASE 18.—When I sell the aforesaid dollars for loss to my creditor;

RULE.—Dr. the Receiver for what I sold them at, Dr. Profit and Loss for my loss on the sale, Cr. Cash by sundries, for their first value.

NOTE.—If my creditor has received the said dollars immediately, the Remitter must be made Cr. instead of Cash.

THE WHOLE COST OF INSURANCE.

CASE 19.—When goods of my own, that were insured, are cast away at sea;

RULE.—Dr. the Insurer, Cr. Voyage to ———.

CASE 20.—When goods of my own, that were not insured, are cast away at sea;

RULE.—Dr. Profit and Loss, Cr. Voyage to ———.

CASE 21.—When the insurance is paid to me before I enter the circumstances in my books;

RULE.—Dr. Cash, Cr. Voyage to ———.

CASE 22.—When the insurance is paid to me after I have entered it;

RULE—Dr. Cash, Cr. the Insurer.

CASE 23.—When I hear of another man's goods insured by me, being cast away, and pay the adventurer immediately;

RULE.—Dr. Insurance, Cr. the Adventurer, and Dr. the Adventurer for the amount of Cash paid him.

CASE 24.—When I hear of another man's goods insured by me, being cast away, and I do not pay the adventurer immediately;

RULE.—Dr. Insurance, Cr. the Adventurer.

GOODS WHEREIN MY FACTOR IS CONCERNED FOR ME.

CASE 25.—When my factor buys goods for my account, or I send goods to him to be disposed of for me;

198 Compendium of Merchants' Accounts.

Rule.—Dr. such Goods in the hands of such factor, or else Voyage to —— for prime cost and charges, Cr. such Factor or Voyage.

Case 26.—When those goods are sold ;

Rule.—Dr. the Factor's Account Current, Cr. Voyage to ——, or else, Cr. Goods in the hands of such factor.

Note.—An account current is that by which an agent balances or makes even with his employer.

Case 27.—When abatements are made on the above said goods, through defects afterwards found ;

Rule.—Dr. Profit and Loss, Cr. Factor's Account Current.

Note.—The same for bad debts, charges of remittances, &c.

Case 28.—When goods of mine, in the hands of one factor, are sent to another factor ;

Rule.—Dr. Voyage to —— (the place of the latter or receiving factor), Cr. the former or sending Factor.

Case 29.—When I receive goods in return from my factor ;

Rule.—Dr. those Goods, Cr. the Factor's Account Current, for prime cost and charges, as per invoice, by double columns, viz., for the foreign money and the currency.

Case 30.—When I pay charges on the above goods ;

Rule.—Dr. those Goods, Cr. Cash.

MONEY BETWEEN ME AND MY FACTOR.

Case 31.—When I draw bills of exchange upon my factor, and receive the contents presently ;

Rule.—Dr. Cash, Cr. the Factor's Account Current.

Case 32.—When I draw bills of exchange upon my factor, and get them accepted, but not received ;

Rule.—Dr. Bills Receivable, Cr. the Factor's Account Current.

Case 33.—When the contents of such accepted bills are received by me some time afterwards ;

Rule.—Dr. Cash, Cr. Bills Receivable.

Case 34.—When my factor draws bills of exchange upon me for goods, bought by him abroad, and I pay the contents presently ;

Compendium of Merchants' Accounts.

Rule.—Dr. the Drawer, Cr. Cash.

Case 35.—When I accept the bills, as above, but do not pay them presently ;

Rule.—Dr. the Drawer, Cr. Bills Payable.

Case 36.—When I pay those accepted bills afterwards ;

Rule.—Dr. Bills Payable, Cr. Cash.

Case 37.—When I remit money to my factor for goods by him sent to me ;

Rule.—Dr. such Factor, Cr. Cash.

Case 38.—When bills of exchange are drawn by one of my factors on another ;

Rule.—Dr. the Factor drawing, Cr. the Factor drawn on ; charging and discharging in such coin as the bills were received and paid in.

Case 39.—When bills of exchange are drawn by one of my factors on another, and the money remitted to me, which I receive immediately ;

Rule.—Dr. Cash, Cr. the factor drawing.

Case 40.—When bills of exchange are drawn by one of my factors on another, and I receive the contents at usance ;

Rule.—Dr. the Acceptor, Cr. Factor drawing.

Case 41.—When I have money in my hands to negotiate with, and deliver it for bills of exchange ;

Rule.—Dr. Account of exchanges, Cr. Cash.

Case 42.—When I dispose of those bills for money ;

Rule.—Dr. Cash, Cr. Account of Exchanges.

Case 43.—When I pay bills of exchange in honor of the drawer or indorser ;

Rull.—Dr. such Drawer or Indorser to sundries, Cr. Cash for the principal and charges, Cr. Profit and Loss for the commission.

OF FACTORAGE ACCOUNTS

I. DOMESTIC.

Case 1.—When I pay charges on goods received on commission ;

Rule.—Dr. Goods for the account of ——, Cr. Cash.

Case 2.—When I sell goods on commission for ready money;

Rule.—Dr. Cash, Cr. Goods for the account of ——.

Case 3.—When I sell goods on commission for trust;

Rule.—Dr. the Buyer, Cr. Goods for the account of ——.

Case 4.—When I sell goods on commission, for part ready money, and part trust;

Rule.—Dr. the Buyer for what he owes, Dr. Cash for what is received, Cr. Goods for the account of —— by sundries.

Case 5.—When I barter goods on commission for other goods;

Rule.—Dr. the Goods bought, Cr. Goods for the account of ——.

Case 6.—When I send goods of my own to my employer, with the charges paid on shipping them;

Rule.—Dr. Goods for the account of —— to sundries, or, Dr. my Employer's Account Current to sundries, Cr. the Goods sent out, Cr. Cash for the charges.

Case 7.—When I buy goods for ready money, and send them directly to my employer, with the charges paid on them;

Rule.—Dr. my Employer's Account Current, Cr. Cash for the principal and charges.

Case 8.—When I buy goods upon trust, and send them directly to my employer, with the charges paid on them;

Rule.—Dr. Goods for the account of —— to sundries, or, Dr. my Employer's Account Current to sundries, Cr. Seller for their value, Cr. Cash for the charges.

Case 9.—When bills are drawn on me by my employer for goods sold, and are payable at usance;

Rule.—Dr. Employer's Account Current, or goods for the account of ——, Cr. Bills Payable.

Case 10.—When I pay the said bill presently;

Rule.—Dr. the Employer's Account Current, or Goods for the account of ——, Cr. Cash.

Note.—The same is to be observed when money is remitted by me to my employer before he draws on me.

Compendium of Merchants' Accounts.

CASE 11.—When goods on commission are all sold, and value handed to the employer, how must the account be closed?

RULE.—Dr. those Goods to sundries, Cr. Cash for payment, and also for the further charges on them, as porterage, cartage, &c., Cr. Profit and Loss for commission and warehouse-room.

II. FOREIGN.

CASE 1.—Goods in my possession sent to my factor by order of my employer;

RULE.—Dr. Voyage to ——, consigned to ——, for the account of —— (my employer), to sundries, Cr. Goods for the account of —— (my employer), Cr. Cash for the charges.

CASE 2.—When those goods are insured, and I pay the premium presently;

RULE.—Dr. Voyage to ——, consigned to ——, for the account of —— (my employer), Cr. Cash.

CASE 3.—When I do not pay the premium till afterwards;

RULE.—Dr. Voyage to —— (as above), Cr. the insurer.

CASE 4.—When I receive advice from my factor, that the goods sent to him from my employer are sold;

RULE.—Dr. such Factor for my employer's account, Cr. Voyage to ——, for the account of —— (my employer).

CASE 5.—When my factor informs me that he has made an abatement for defects, &c., found afterwards;

RULE.—Dr. Voyage to ——, for the account of —— (my employer), Cr. such Factor for the account of —— (my employer).

CASE 6.—When goods are returned to me from my factor, for goods sold by him for my employer;

RULE.—Dr. the Goods received for the account of my employer, Cr. that Factor for the account of my employer.

CASE 7.—When I pay charges thereon;

RULE.—Dr. Goods received for the account of my employer, Cr. Cash.

CASE 8.—When goods returned from my factor are consigned directly from him to my employer;

RULE.—Dr. such Employer's Account Current, Cr. Factor for my employer's account.

CASE 9.—When commission is due to me from my employer, for goods sold by my factor;

RULE.—Dr. Voyage to ——, for account of —— (my employer), Cr. Profit and Loss.

CASE 10.—When I make abatements afterwards, and for bad debts;

RULE.—Dr. Factor's Account Current, Cr. the Person to whom the abatement is made, or whose debt is lost.

CASE 11.—When I pay charges on remittances and postage of letters;

RULE.—Dr. Factor's Account Current, Cr. Cash or Charges of Merchandise.

NOTE.—When goods on commission are all sold, the produce clear of all charges is called the net proceeds, for which Dr. Goods for the account of ——, Cr. Factor's Account Current.

III. COMPANY ACCOUNT.

MYSELF KEEPING THE ACCOUNT, AND HAVING THE DISPOSAL OF THE GOODS.

CASE 1.—When goods in company are bought by me for ready money;

RULE.—Dr. those Goods for the cost and charges (if there be any), Cr. Cash.

CASE 2.—When goods in company are bought by me on trust;

RULE.—Dr. those goods for the cost and charges (if there be any), Cr. the Seller.

CASE 3.—When goods in company are sold by me for ready money;

RULE.—Dr. Cash, Cr. Goods in Company.

CASE 4.—When goods in company are sold by me on trust;

RULE.—Dr. the Buyer, Cr. Goods in Company, Cr. his Account Current

Compendium of Merchants' Accounts.   203

CASE 5.—When goods in company are sold to myself;

RULE.—Dr. those Goods for proper account, Cr. Goods in Company.

CASE 6.—When goods in company are sold to my partner;

RULE.—Dr. his Account Current, Cr. Goods in Company, Cr. his Account Current.

CASE 7.—When goods in company are sold by me for part ready money and part trust ;

RULE.—Cr. Cash for what is received, Dr. the Buyer for what remains due, Cr. Goods in Company by sundries for the full value.

CASE 8.—When goods of my own are brought into company ;

RULE.—Dr. Goods in Company, Cr. Goods proper.

CASE 9.—When the whole is furnished by me ;

RULE.—Dr. Goods in Company, Cr. the Seller if bought on trust, Cr. Cash if bought for present money.

CASE 10.—When goods of my partner are brought into company;

RULE.—Dr. Goods in Company, Cr. Partner's Account.

CASE 11.—When the whole is furnished by my partner;

RULE.—Dr. Goods in Company, Cr. Partner's Account Current for the whole.

CASE 12.—When goods in company are all sold; if there be gain ;

RULE.—Dr. the Goods in Company to sundries, Cr. Partner's Account for his share, Cr. Profit and Loss for my share.

CASE 13.—When goods in company are all sold ; if there be loss ;

RULE.—Dr. Partner's Account for his share of the loss, Dr. Profit and Loss for my share, Cr. the Goods in Company by sundries.

CASE 14.—When goods in company are sent over sea to be sold, I paying the charges ;

RULE.—Dr. Voyage to —— in Company to sundries for the whole charge, Cr. Goods in Company for their value, Cr. Cash for the charges.

Case 15.—When I buy goods for company account with ready money, and ship them off, paying the charges of the shipping ;

Rule.—Dr. Voyage in Company for the whole charge, Cr. Cash for the same sum.

Case 16.—When I buy goods for company account on trust, and ship them off before they are entered in my Ledger, paying the charges of shipping ;

Rule.—Dr. Voyage to —— in Company to sundries, for the whole charges, Cr. the Seller for the prime cost, Cr. Cash for the after-charges.

Case 17.—When I receive goods from our factor for company account, in return for goods sent and sold, with charges paid by me at the receipt thereof ;

Rule.—Dr. Goods received in Company to sundries, for their prime cost and charges, Cr. Factor at —— for company account, for the cost and charges, as per invoice, Cr. Cash for the charges paid at their receipt.

Case 18.—When goods are sent from my factor in one place, to our factor in another ;

Rule.—Dr. Voyage to ——, consigned to our factor, Cr. my Factor at —— his Account Current.

Case 19.—When goods are sent by our factor in one place to my factor in another place, in return for goods sold for company account ;

Rule.—Dr. Voyage to ——, consigned to ——, my factor at ——, Cr. our Factor at ——

Case 20.—When goods are sold by our factor as per his advice ;

Rule.—Dr. Factor at —— his Account Current, Cr. Voyage to —— in Company.

Case 21.—When I receive advice that my factor has afterwards made some abatement ;

Rule.—Dr. Voyage to ——, Cr. Factor at —— his Account Current.

Case 22.—When I receive money of my partner for his share of goods formerly bought ;

Compendium of Merchants' Accounts.

Rule.—Dr. Cash, Cr. Partner's Account Current.

Case 23.—When money is remitted to me by our Factor for goods sold;

Rule.—Dr. Cash, Cr. Factor at —— his Account Current.

Case 24.—When money is remitted to me by our Factor for goods sold, but payable at usance;

Rule.—Dr. Bills Receivable, Cr. Factor at —— his Account Current.

Case 25.—When I pay money on sight of my partner's bill;

Rule.—Dr. Partner's Account Current, Cr. Cash.

Case 26.—When I give to my creditor a bill on my partner, for his share of the goods in company;

Rule.—Dr. the Receiver of the Bill, *i. e.*, my Creditor, Cr. Partner's Account Current.

MY PARTNER KEEPING THE ACCOUNT, AND HAVING THE DISPOSAL OF THE GOODS.

Case 1.—When I pay my share in money;

Rule.—Dr. the Company, Cr. Cash.

Case 2.—When I furnish my share in goods;

Rule.—Dr. the Company, Cr. the Goods.

Case 3.—When I furnish both my own and my partner's share;

Rule.—Dr. the Company for my share, Dr. Partner's Account Current for his share, Cr. the Goods by sundries.

Case 4.—When my partner furnishes my share as well as his own;

Rule.—Dr. the Company, Cr. Partner's Account Current for my share only.

Case 5.—When my partner sends me an account of the sale of goods in company;

Rule.—Dr. Partner's Account Current, Cr. the Company for my share of the net proceeds.

Case 6.—If there be gain on the above sale;

Rule.—Dr. the Company, Cr. Profit and Loss.

Case 7.—If there be loss ;

Rule.—Dr. Profit and Loss, Cr. the Company.

Case 8.—When my partner draws on me for my share of goods in company, and I pay the same presently ;

Rule.—Dr. Partner's Account Current, Cr. Cash.

Case 9.—When my partner draws on me as above at usance,

Rule.—Dr. Partner's Account Current, Cr. Bills Payable.

The General Balance of the Whole Ledger, in order to Transfer the same into New Books.

OBSERVE 1.—All accounts are balanced either by Balance or by Profit and Loss, except Accounts in Company, which are balanced by the Goods in Partnership for my partner's gain, or to these Goods for his loss thereon.

OBSERVE 2.—When accounts with persons are made even by receipts or payments, those accounts stand balanced already.

OBSERVE 3.—When accounts remain unfinished :—

CASE 1.—If it be of money remaining in hand ;
RULE.—Dr. Account of Balance, Cr. Cash.

CASE 2.—If it be of persons who are debtors ;
RULE.—Dr. Account of Balance, Cr. their Accounts.

CASE 3.—If it be of persons who are creditors ;
RULE.—Dr. their Accounts, Cr. Balance.

CASE 4.—If it be of goods which are all sold, and there is gain ;
RULE.—Dr. those Goods, Cr. Profit and Loss.

CASE 5.—If it be of goods which are all sold, and there is loss ;
RULE.—Dr. Profit and Loss, Cr. those Goods.

CASE 6.—If it be of goods, part sold and part unsold ;
RULE.—For what is sold Dr. and Cr. as above ; for what is unsold, Dr. Balance, Cr. the goods at prime cost.

NOTE.—The same when all the goods remain unsold.

OBSERVE 4.—The accounts of Insurance, charges of Merchandise, Interest, House expenses, &c., are all balanced by Profit and Loss.

OBSERVE 5.—The Accounts of Profit and Loss and Balance are balanced by Stock, they being made Drs. to or Crs. by Stock, as their particular balances direct.

OBSERVE 6.—The account of Stock is balanced by the several balances of Profit and Loss, and Balance being brought thereto.

OBSERVE 7.—The account of Balance in the old books will be the Inventory of the new ones.

APPENDIX.

APPENDIX.

ARITHMETICAL RULES.

EQUATION OF PAYMENTS—AVERAGES.

RULE—(1.) Multiply each of the debts, except that which is earliest due, by the difference of the days, or time, between its date and that of each successive one. (2.) Divide the sum of these products by the sum of the debts, and add the quotient thus obtained to the date of the first debt; these days counted forward will give date of average note.

EXAMPLE.

A. B. makes the following purchases from C. D., @ 4 months, from the undermentioned dates, viz., Jan. 3rd, $500 ; February 12th, $300, and March the 29th, $600 :—

Jan. 3rd.... 500
Feb. 12th . 300 × 40 (Number of days from 3rd Jan. to 12th Feb.) = 12,000
Mar. 29th . 600 × 85 (Number of days from 3rd Jan. to 29th Mar.) = 51,000

The sum of the debts...$1400   The sum of the products of the debts and days.......... 63,000

63000 ÷ 1400 = 45 the quotient.

Add the 45 days thus formed to 3rd January, the date of the first debt, 45 + 3 = 48 days, which, counted forward, will give 17th February, the date of Average note for $1400 ; of course the note will be due 4 months from this date, viz., the 17th and 20th June.

RULES FOR REDUCING STERLING MONEY TO HALIFAX AND DECIMAL CURRENCY AND VICE VERSA.

FIRST.—TO REDUCE STERLING TO HALIFAX CURRENCY.

RULE.—To the sterling add one-fifth of itself and one-twelfth of that fifth.

SECOND—TO REDUCE HALIFAX CURRENCY TO DECIMAL CURRENCY.

RULE.—(1.) Multiply the £s by 4, adding the fives of the shillings as units of Dollars, if there be so many. (2.)* Multiply the remaining shillings (if any) by 20, and the pence by $\frac{5}{3}$ for cents.

† EXAMPLE I.

	£500	10	0	Stg. to Halifax Cy. Rule 1st.
$\frac{1}{5}$	100	2	0	
$\frac{1}{12}$	8	6	10	
	£608	18	10	Halifax Cy. Reduce to $s. Rule 2nd.
	4			
	$2435	$76\frac{2}{3}$		Decimal Cy.

THIRD.—TO REDUCE STERLING TO DECIMAL CURRENCY DIRECT.

RULE.—Multiply the £s by 4.86\frac{2}{3}$, adding the aliquot parts of the Shillings and Pence taken on the multiplier.

EXAMPLE II.

	£500 10 0		Stg. to Decimal Cy. direct.
	$4.86\frac{2}{3}$		
	3000		
	4000		
	2000		
	$1.66\frac{2}{3}$	=	$\frac{2}{3}$ of 500
	$1.66\frac{2}{3}$		
10s. = $\frac{1}{2}$	$2.43\frac{1}{3}$	=	$\frac{1}{2}$ of $4.86\frac{2}{3}$
	$2435 $76\frac{2}{3}$		Same as above.

* The multiplication by 20, and by $\frac{5}{3}$ should be performed mentally, as in the example.

† I prefer the mode of operation Exemplified in the first Example, to the second, although it were only required to reduce the Stg. to Decimal Cy., and not to Halifax as well. The work is much more intricate by the second method, especially when the shillings and pence in the Stg. would necessiate the taking of many aliquot parts.

APPENDIX.

FOURTH.—TO REDUCE DECIMAL CURRENCY TO HALIFAX CURRENCY AND STERLING.

RULE.—(1.) Divide the Decimal Cy. by 4 for Halifax Cy. (2.) By proportion, to reduce the Halifax Cy. to Stg.

EXAMPLES.

$2435.76⅔ Decimal Cy. ÷ 4* = £608 18 10 Halifax Cy.
(2.) As 73 : 60 : : £608 18 10 Halifax Cy. to Stg.

```
              6
        ─────────
        3653 13  0
              10
        ─────────
   73)36530 10  0(£500 10  0 Stg.
      365..
      ─────
         36
         20
       ─────
        730
         73.
        ────
          0
          0
        ────
          ||
```

FIFTH.—TO REDUCE DECIMAL CURRENCY TO STERLING DIRECT.

RULE.—Divide the amount, Decimal Cy., by $4.86⅔

EXAMPLE.

$2435.76⅔ Decimal Cy. ÷ 4.86⅔ = £500 10 0 sterling.
Or thus :—

```
   4.86⅔)$2435.76⅔ ÷ $4.86⅔
      3          3
   ─────────────────────
   1460) 7307.30(£500 10  0 Stg.
         7300..
         ──────
            730
             20
           ─────
          14600
          1460.
          ─────
              0
              0
           ─────
             ||
```

---

* In the division by 4 consider the units of the remaining dollars, if any, as fives of Shillings; and the twenties in the cents, if any, as units of the Shillings, and add them together for the shillings of the answer, and Multiply the remaining cents, if any, by 3·5 for pence. This operation should also be performed mentally.

APPENDIX. 213

SIMPLE INTEREST.

RULE 1.—To find the interest of a given sum for a year, at a given rate per cent. per annum. Multiply the principal by the rate, and divide the product by 100.

EXAMPLE.

Required the interest on $375, for 1 year, at 8 per cent. per annum.

$375 × 8 ÷ 100 = 30\frac{00}{100}$, interest for one year.

RULE 2.—To find the interest of a given principal for any number of Months. Find the interest for a year by rule 1, and take aliquot parts for the months.

EXAMPLE 1

Required the interest (for a greater time than a year), on $800, for 15 months, at 7 per cent. per annum.

$800 × 7 ÷ 100 = 56$\frac{00}{100}$, interest for 1 year; find the ¼ of this amount, and add it to it, for the additional 3 months; therefore, $56 + 14 = 70\frac{00}{100}$, the interest for 15 months.

EXAMPLE 2

Required the interest (for a less time than a year), on $500, for 9 months, at 7 per cent. per annum.

$500 × 7 ÷ 100 = 35$\frac{00}{100}$, interest for 1 year; the ¾ of which will be the interest for 9 months; therefore, $35 × ¾ = $26.25, interest for 9 months.

RULE 3.—To find the interest of a given sum for any number of days. Multiply the principal by twice the rate, and the product by the days, and divide the result by 73,000.

EXAMPLE.

Required the interest on $1000, for 40 days, at 6 per cent. per annum.

$1000 × 12 × 40 ÷ 73,000 = 6.57\frac{31}{73}$, interest.

EXCHANGE.

(1.) To find the value of any sum—U. S. Currency in gold, (or Canadian Currency.)

RULE.—Multiply the number of dollars of U. S. Currency by 100, and divide the product by the price of gold in greenbacks; the quotient will be the number of dollars in gold, or (Canadian Currency).

214   APPENDIX.

EXAMPLE.—When gold sells at 140, what is the value of 2100\frac{00}{100}$, U. S. Currency?

$2100 × 100 ÷ 140 = 1500\frac{00}{100}$, answer, in gold (or Canadian Cy.)

(2.) To find the value of any sum—gold (or Canadian Cy.) in U. S. Cy. (or greenbacks), at any given rate of discount.

RULE.—Multiply the number of dollars in gold (or Canadian Cy.) by 100, and divide the product by 100 less the discount.

EXAMPLE.—Find the value of $1200 gold (or Canadian Cy.) in U. S. Currency, discount on the latter @ 25 per cent.

$1200.00 × 100 ÷ 75 = $1600.00, answer, in U. S. Currency.

RULES TO DETERMINE THE VALUE OF GOODS ON HAND AT THE TIME OF A FIRE.

RULE 1ST.

When the advance on the prime cost is an aliquot part of $100, as 50 per cent. = ½, 75 per cent. = ¾.

To the denominator of the fraction, indicating the aliquot part, add the numerator; thus, $\frac{1}{2}+\frac{1}{1}=\frac{1}{3}$; $\frac{3}{4}+\frac{3}{3}=\frac{3}{7}$, &c. And subtract from the total sales the amount expressed by the fraction, whose denominator has been thus increased, to determine the prime cost of the goods sold. This amount subtracted from the amount of the goods purchased will give the prime cost of the goods on hand at the time of the fire.

EXAMPLE AT 12½ PER CENT. OR ⅛.

A. B. purchases, at various times, goods amounting to $50,000, and his sales amount to $54,000, including advance: then $\frac{1}{8}+\frac{1}{1}=\frac{1}{9}$ of $54,000 = $6,000, which subtract from $54,000 = $48,000, the prime cost of the goods sold; which deduct from the amount purchased, $50,000 = $2,000, the amount of goods on hand at time of fire.

RULE 2ND.

When the per cent. advance is not an aliquot part of $100; then as $100, plus the per cent. advance is to $100; so is the amount of goods sold to the prime cost.

EXAMPLE AT 17 PER CENT. ADVANCE.

Let the amount of goods purchased be $40,000, and the amount of sales $35,100:—then as $100 + 17 : $100 : : $35,100; or, as $117 : $100 : : $35,100 : $30,000. The fourth term, viz. $30,000 = the prime cost of goods sold; subtract this amount from the $40,000 purchased, and we have $10,000, value of goods on hand at time of fire.

APPENDIX.

INVOICE.

INVOICE of 300 barrels Beef, and 400 barrels Pork, Shipped by A. V. Delaporte, on board the barque "New Dominion," John Fairweather, master, for Liverpool, on account and risk of William Brown & Co., there.

		$	c.
W.B. L.	300 barrels Mess Beef, @ $16\frac{00}{100}$	4800	00
	400 do. do Pork, @ $18\frac{00}{100}$	7200	00
		12000	00
	CHARGES :		
	CARTAGE, WHARFAGE, and SHIPPING	20	00
	COMMISSION ON $12000, @ 2½ per cent	300	00
	INSURANCE (F.P.A.)* on $12320, @ 3 pr. ct...	369	60
		12689	60

Errors Excepted.

A. V. DELAPORTE.

Toronto, 1st June, 1868.

The following are the usual Modes of Effecting Marine Insurance :—

1. *F.P.A. Means "Free From Particular Average," and the party so insuring, in case of loss or damage of cargo, shall receive amount of loss.

2. P.A. Means "Particular Average," and signifies that the party insuring—insures for only a proportion of loss, say, 5, 10, or 20 per cent.

3. G.A. Means "General Average," and signifies that all the parties' insurances, on the particular cargo, pay their proportion of the loss.

APPENDIX.

FORM OF ACCOUNT CURRENT*

WITH MODE OF CALCULATING THE INTEREST THEREON AT—SAY SIX PER CENT. PER ANNUM.

Dr.   A. Jardine in Account Current with John Jones.   Cr.

1868.			$	c.	1868.			$	c.
Feb.	10	To Goods	931	50	Mar.	24	By Goods	832	67
,,	25	,, ,, ...	1072	00	April	6	,, Cash	1738	60
June	20	,, ,, ...	2076	67	Sept.	26	,, Bill on Cary & Co	1000	00
Dec.	10	,, Interest (see below)	37	44	Dec.	10	,, Balance	546	34
			4117	61				4117	61

DR.   CR.

February 10th....$ 931 50 × 304 = 282176 00
,,   25th....   1072 00 × 289 = 309808 00
June 20th........ 2076 67 × 173 = 359263 91
March 24th ......   832 67 × 261 = ... $217326 87
April 6th .... 1738 60 × 248 = ...   431172 80
September 26th .. 1000 00 × 75 = ...   75000 00
                                   ———————   ———————
                                    951247 91   723499 67
                                    723499 67
                                   ———————
                                    227748 24

By former Rule for Interest, multiply 227748.24 by twice the rate, and divide by 73,000:

227748.24 × 12 ÷ 73,000 = $37.44 interest, as against Jardine.

---

* An Account Current contains a statement of the mercantile transactions of one person with another, when immediate payments are not made. It is usually written on two pages, marked Dr. and Cr. in the manner of a Ledger Account, the left hand page containing the payments made by the merchant who furnishes the Account, and the other what is paid to him.

APPENDIX. 217

FORMS OF BILLS.

PROMISSORY NOTE.

Toronto, June 1st, 1868.

$1000.00

  Four months after date, I* promise to pay to John Jones & Co., one thousand dollars, at the Royal Canadian Bank here, value received.

         JAMES JOHNSON.
No. 1.

DRAFT.

Toronto, June 1st, 1868.

$500.00

  Sixty days after date, pay to my order at the Gore Bank, Hamilton, five hundred dollars, value received.

         JNO. ROGERS.

John White, Esq., Galt.

BILL OF EXCHANGE.

Toronto, June 1st, 1868.

£350 *Sterling.*

  Thirty days after sight of this, first of Exchange, (second and third unpaid,) pay to the order of Pickford & Co., London, three hundred and fifty pounds sterling, value received.

         CLARKSON & Co.

To Messrs. Baring & Co.,
  London.

---

*If a note is to be signed by a firm or more than one person, write We instead of I.

P

APPENDIX.

ABBREVIATIONS AND CHARACTERS

USED IN THIS WORK.

ABBREVIATIONS.

Ac't....Account.	Emb'd..Embroidered.	Mo.....Month.
Am't....Amount.	Ex.....Example.	M......Thousand.
Ans....Answer.	Exch....Exchange.	
Apr....April.	Exp....Expenses.	No......Number.
Ass't'd..Assorted.		Nov....November.
Aug....August.	Fav.....Favor.	
	Feb.....February.	Oct.....October.
Bal....Balance.	Fig'd....Figured.	O.I.B...Outward Invoice Book.
B.B....Bill Book.	Fol.....Folio.	
Bbls....Barrels.	For'd....Forward.	p.......Page.
B.P....Bills Payable.	Fr't....Freight.	Pay't....Payment.
B.R....Bills Receivable.	F.C.B..Folio Cash Book	P.C.B..Petty Cash Book
Blk....Black.	F.O.B..Free on Board.	Pd.....Paid.
Bo't....Bought.	F.P.A..Free from particular average.	Pkg.....Package.
Bro't....Brought.		Pr......Pair.
	Gal.....Gallon.	pr., per..By.
Cy.....Currency.	G A....General average	Prem....Premium.
Cap.....Capital.		P.A....Particular average.
C.B....Cash Book.	Hhd....Hogshead.	
Co......Company.		P.D.B..Page Day Book
Com....Commission.	I.B.....Invoice Book.	P.W.B..Page Waste Book.
Const....Consignment.	Ins.....Insurance	
Cr......Creditor.	Inst....Instant.	qr......Quarter.
C,O.D..Cash on delivery	Int......Interest.	
Cwt....Hundred weight	Inv.....Invoice.	Rec'd....Received.
	Inv't....Inventory.	
Dec.....December.	i.e......That is.	S.B.....Sales Book.
D'ft....Draft.		Sept.....September.
Disct....Discount.	Jan....January.	Ship't...Shipment.
do......The same.	J.F.....Journal Folio.	Sunds...Sundries.
doz.....Dozen.		
Dr......Debtor.	lbs......Pounds.	viz......Videlicet.
d's......Days.	L.F....Ledger Folio.	
ea......Each.	Mar....March.	Yds.....Yards.
E. E....Errors Excepted	Mdse....Merchandise.	Yr......Year.

CHARACTERS.

ac't..Account.	s. ..Shilling.	= Sign of Equality.
@ ..At or to.	d. ..Pence.	1-4 One-fourth.
% ..Per Cent.	✓ ..Check Mark.	1-2 One-half.
$ ..Dollars.	+ Sign of Addition.	1-3 One-third.
c. ..Cents.	— Sign of Subtraction.	3-5 Three-fifths.
℔ ..Per.	× Sign of Multiplicat'n.	5-3 Five-thirds.
£ ..Pound Sterling.	÷ Sign of Division.	1-16 One-sixteenth.

APPENDIX.

A SHORT
EXPLANATION
OF
COMMERCIAL TERMS OR EXPRESSIONS.

(Extracted from Morrison's Book-keeping.)

Accommodation, when applied to Bills or Notes, are those for which no value has been given ; that is, when the Drawee only lends his name ; and that the Drawer engages to provide him with the means of payment when the bill falls due.

Adventure, when a merchant exports goods to or from a foreign market on his own account and risk, it is called an individual speculation, or adventure to or from that place.

Advice, mercantile intelligence ; to advise a bill is to describe the amount, date, term, to whom payable, etc., and to request the person on whom drawn to accept it.

Affidavit, signifies an oath in writing, sworn before some person who is authorized to take the same.

Agent, a person duly empowered to do business for another.

Arbitration, the determination of a cause by persons mutually chosen by the parties.

Assignee, a person deputed by another to manage the subject of a bankrupt.

Average, a contribution made for losses at sea, which falls upon the proprietors or insurers in a just proportion.

Balance of Trade, the difference between the commercial exports and imports of one country with respect to another.

Bank Bill, a bill drawn on and accepted by a banking-house or banker.

Bankrupt, a trader whom misfortune or extravagance has rendered unable to pay his debts.

Barter, the trucking or exchanging of one commodity for another.

Bills on the circle, those under acceptance, and which we are bound to pay.

Bills in hand, those which we have in hand, and for which we receive payment.

Bill of Entry, a list of the particulars of goods entered at the Custom-house.

Bill of Lading, a printed agreement between the shipper of goods and the captain of a ship, binding the latter to deliver them "in good order and well-conditioned," on payment of a certain freight. It is usual to make out three bills, one to the shipper, the second to be held by the captain, and the third to be sent to the person to whom the goods are consigned, by which he can claim them on their arrival.

Bill of Sale is a solemn contract, under seal, whereby a person conveys the right and interest which he has in goods and chattels.

Bill of Store is a license granted by the Custom-house to merchants, to carry such stores and provisions as are necessary for a voyage, free of duty.

Blank Credit, the permission which one house gives to another to draw on it to a certain extent, at any time, for their own accommodation.

Broker, an agent employed by merchants in buying and selling, who, for a trifling charge, finds the merchant buyers in one case, and sellers in the other. There are several kinds of Brokers, such as Ship-Brokers, Insurance-Brokers, Exchange-Brokers, Stock-Brokers, etc.

Bonded Goods are certain articles which, on being landed, are warehoused upon bond being given by the owner for the payment of duties, etc.

Bottomry is a contract in the nature of a mortgage of a ship, when the owner of it borrows money to enable him to carry on a voyage, and pledges the keel or *bottom* of the ship as a security for the repayment; and it is understood that it the vessel be lost, the lender loses the money.

Bounty is a premium paid by Government to the exporters of certain British commodities to foreign parts, &c. *See Debenture.*

Brokerage is a commission or ℔ Centage paid by merchants to brokers, either for the sale or purchase of goods, bills of exchange, stock, &c.

Capital or *Stock*, the effects of a house in money or wares, by means of which it carries on trade and supports it credit.

Charter Party, the engagement between the owner of a ship and the merchant, who engages the whole ship to go from one port to another with goods, for a certain sum.

Chevisance, a composition between Debtor and Creditor.

Circulating Medium, cash, bank-notes or other paper money, payable on demand.

Circular Letter, the printed notice of the establishment or dissolution of a house, or alteration in the firm, &c. *See Firm.*

Cocket, a Custom-house warrant given on the entry of goods for exportation, to signify they have paid the duty.

Commission, an allowance given to agents or factors for transacting the business of others, always so much ℔ Cent.

Commission of Bankruptcy, an order under the great seal, directing five or more Commissioners to inquire into the affairs of a bankrupt.

Composition, part of a debt taken in lieu of the whole.

Compromise, to adjust a dispute by mutual concessions.

Consignment, goods sent by one house to another to sell for their account, allowing them so much ℔ Cent. for their trouble. *See Commission.*

Contraband Trade, that which is prohibited by law.

Contingent, the proportion that falls to the share of a person concerned in any business or adventure.

Convoy, ships of war sailing with other ships, in order to protect them.

Counter-Order, an order, sent to revoke a former one, either for the sale or purchase of any commodity.

Credit, in general, the confidence which one house reposes in another; more particularly, the reverse of *Debit*.

Currency, the money in circulation, as distinguished from bank-paper, &c.

Current, a term used to express the present time. Hence the *Price Current* of any merchandise is the known or ordinary price at the time it is published.

Custom-house, where entries are made on goods exported or imported, and the duties imposed by law paid.

Debentures, a certificate given by the proper officers of the customs on certain goods exported, on which the exporter or seller is entitled to a drawback or bounty.

Del Credere, a ℔ Centage made by merchants in selling goods for guaranteeing the solidity of the purchaser.

Demurrage, a penalty incurred by merchants for delaying a ship beyond the time specified in her charter-party.

Deviation, is a departure, without legal cause, from the regular course of a voyage, which deviation incapaciates the insured from recovering in case of loss.

Dishonor, an expression made use of when bills of exchange, &c., are refused acceptance or payment.

Dividend, a share of any capital, debt, or profit; also the interest in the stocks.

Drawback, a premium allowed on exportations. *See Debenture.*

Dubious paper, means bills drawn on houses of little credit.

Due protection, regular acceptance or payment of a draft or bill.

Duty, the tax imposed by Government upon the import or export of goods.

Effects, monies, goods, or moveables in the hands of one person belonging to another.

Embargo, an arrest on ships or merchandise by public authority.

Emporium, a principal place for the importation and sale of merchandise.

Excise is an inland charge or imposition on various commodities.

Factorage, called also Commission, is an allowance to factors by those who employ them.

APPENDIX. 221

Finances, a term generally applied to the public revenues.

Firm, the mercantile appellation of a house engaged in commerce.

First-rate Paper, bills drawn or accepted by a good house, such as has always paid its bills regularly

Flat, an article of merchandise is said to be flat when there are few buyers.

Freight, the sum paid for transporting merchandise by sea, &c.

Gazette, a paper published by Government, containing, among other things, notices of the dissolution of partnerships, commissioners of bankruptcy, suspension or continuance of bounties, embargoes, &c.

Government, "for your government," is an expression adopted from the French signifying, "in order to give you better information, and rules for acting by, in the purchase or sale of any merchandise."

Guarantee, a person who undertakes that certain stipulations shall be fulfilled.

Honor, to honor a draft is to accept it on presentation.

Impost, a certain tax or duty levied on merchandise imported.

Insolvent, a tradesman who has not a capital adequate to the payment of his debts is said to be insolvent.

Instalments, payments of a debt in certain proportions, and at stipulated times.

Insurance or *Assurance* is a contract of indemnity, by which one party engages, for a stipulated sum, to insure another against a risk to which he is exposed. The party who takes upon him the risk, is called the *Insurer* or *Underwriter;* and the party protected by the insurance is called the *Insured;* the sum paid is called the *Premium;* and the instrument containing the contract is called the *Policy.*

Interest, a premium paid for the use or loan of money. To guard a person's interest is to protect his property, and watch over his concerns.

Landwaiter, an officer belonging to the Custom-house, whose duty it is to take an account of goods imported.

Letter of Advice, a letter giving notice of any transaction.

Letter of Attorney, or power of Attorney, a writing which empowers one person therein named to act for another.

Letter of Credit, a letter by which one person receives money or goods on the credit of another.

Letter of License is a written permission granted to a person under embarrassment, allowing him to conduct his affairs for a certain time without molestation.

Letters of Marque, a power granted by the Lords of the Admiralty to ships fitted out by individuals to act against the common enemy.

License, a privilege from Government for carrying on a trade or business, on which a certain duty is laid.

Lien, a claim or attachment on any property which a person has in his possession, for a debt due to him from the owner of the property.

Lighterage, a charge for carrying goods to and from a ship in a lighter.

Liquidation, is the winding up of a business, such as paying and receiving all debts, &c.

Manifest, a list of a ship's cargo, which paper must be signed by the master of the vessel before any of the goods can be landed.

Maturity, in bills, is when they become due.

Maximum, the highest price of any article, as fixed by some law or regulation.

Minimum, the lowest price of any article, as fixed by some regulation.

Nonclaim is where a creditor neglects to make his claim within a proper time, in which case he cannot enforce his demand.

Notary Public, is a person legally empowered to attest deeds and other writings; also to note and protest bills, drafts, or notes, when refused or returned

Order, a direction from one house to another to effect certain purchases, &c., upon limited or unlimited conditions.

Pass in Conformity, or to state in conformity, is to acknowledge that an account transmitted is correct.

Pierage, money paid for the support of an established pier.

Primage, so much ℔ Cent. generally allowed to the captain of a ship on the amount of freight.

Prime Entry, the first or original entry made at the Custom-house on goods imported or exported.

Price Current, a list of the articles in the market, with the present prices annexed to each, and which is generally furnished every month.

Procuration, the power of using the signature of a house on letters and bills.

Quarantine, the time a ship suspected of infection is restricted from intercourse with the shore; also certain duties imposed on ships.

Quoted on board, means the price for which a merchant agrees to put goods on board, free of expenses of shipping to the buyer.

Remittance, a sum of money sent either in bills of exchange or otherwise, from one house to another.

Renewal of a Bill, is the cancelling a bill or promissory note due, and accepting another at a given date in lieu thereof.

Salvage, a certain allowance due to those through whose instrumentality property is saved from the perils of the seas, enemies, &c.

Solidity, the character which a house bears as to property.

Solvent, a person in trade who is able to pay his debts.

Tidewaiters, officers employed to see the loading and unloading of ships, in order to prevent contraband trade.

Tonnage, the admeasurement of a ship by which she pays the tonnage duty; or it is her actual capacity for stowage, and is in that case not unfrequently called her burthen.

Tonnage, an impost of so much ℔ Ton on liquors imported or exported.

Umpire, when two arbitrators cannot agree in settling a dispute, a third person is named, who is called an *umpire*, and whose decision is binding.

Underwriters, persons who insure ships, cargoes, or other risks, which is performed by writing their names under a policy of insurance.

Usance, time given for payment of bills of exchange.

Usury, * consists in taking more than five ℔ Cent., which is called legal interest, for the loan of money, when the obligation to repay is absolute.

Value, to value, in a mercantile sense, is to draw a bill; the words, "value received," or "value in account," are always mentioned in every bill of exchange.

Wharfage, money paid for the use of a wharf.

---

* That is in England. In Canada six per Cent. is the nominal rate; but the borrower and lender may, however, agree to any r: te they please. Money under this condition may be said to be free in Canada.

TESTIMONIALS
IN FAVOR OF
"THE DOMINION ACCOUNTANT."

PRIVATE TESTIMONIALS.

From Thos. Woodside, Esq., Cashier Royal Canadian Bank, Toronto, 13th Nov. 1868.

I am satisfied the Dominion Accountant will supply a want which has long been felt, viz:—A system of Book-keeping that can be easily understood by any one ignorant of the science or art.
The examples given seem well adapted to the requirements of a learner.
The book is well executed as to its typography, and is remarkably moderate in price. I have no doubt but its merits will command for it a large sale.

From the Rev. John Jennings, D.D., Chairman of the Council of Public Instruction for Ontario, Toronto, 14th Nov., 1868.

In looking through the Dominion Accountant I find I get knowledge; and if any one can be looked to as an authority and teacher, you stand among the very foremost.

From the Rev. Wm. Morley Punshon, M.A., President of the Wesleyan Conference, Toronto, 3rd Dec., 1868.

I have looked over the Dominion Accountant, and think it well calculated to serve the purpose of its publication.

From the Rev. Wm. Gregg, M.A., Toronto, 26th Dec., 1868.

I have looked over the Dominion Accountant, which appears well calculated, from its clearness and conciseness, for the purposes of a text book in Book-keeing.
The questions, notes, and explanations, as well as the rules appended for interest and exchange, I consider particularly useful.

From David Higgins, Esq., Secretary to the Edinburgh Life Assurance Company, Toronto, 29th August, 1870.

I have great pleasure in stating that I consider your "DOMINION ACCOUNTANT" THE BEST WORK ON BOOK-KEEPING I HAVE SEEN IN THE COURSE OF A LONG EXPERIENCE. I highly approve of the various "Sets of Books" shown in it, which exemplify how accounts may be kept, either simply or elaborately, according to the requirements of circumstances. I strongly recommend the work to both Teachers and Students. The former will, I am certain, on inspection, readily appreciate its value, and the latter, even if unable to secure the assistance of an instructor, can, by a careful study of its rules and examples, become acquainted with all the operations and details of Book-keeping, and fully qualify themselves for the duties of an Accountant. I add here that the Definitions and Arithmetical Rules contained in the Book, contribute greatly to its value.

From Andrew Henderson, of the firm of Henderson, Wallace and Company, Toronto, 5th Sept., 1870.

I have carefully examined your "Dominion Accountant," and beg to say that, from an experience of thirty years in Practical Book-keeping, I can confidently state that your system of Book-keeping, as exemplified in the above-mentioned work, single and double entry, is better adapted as a Text Book, or Self Instructor, than any system that ever came under my notice. The Arithmetical Rules in the Appendix are invaluable to Commercial Students.

EXTRACTS FROM THE OPINIONS OF THE PRESS.

From the Toronto Globe.

"THE DOMINION ACCOUNTANT."—Those intending to enter Mercantile life will find this a most valuable instructor. The chief excellence of the work is its simplicity and practicability. The thorough carefulness shown by the author to lead the student gradually from the easier to the more difficult descriptions of accounts, is sure to encourage the most timid beginner. Bankers and mercantile men have given it recommendations as a treatise that surpasses any they have yet seen for its adaptation to the school and the counting-room.

From the Toronto Leader, 11th Nov., 1868.

The work before us is more progressive in its plan than any with which we have yet met. It lays the foundation of a practical knowledge of Book-keeping. We recommend this volume to accountants, in whatever business they may be engaged; they will find it very valuable as a book of reference, and it is so arranged that at any point in their progress they can find an exact counterpart, and by turning to it may at once verify their work.

From the Guelph Mercury.

The treatise is a very able one on the subject, and if the Board of Education would authorise its introduction into the schools it would be fortunate for the pupils. The author has brought to the task of producing the Dominion Accountant a large measure of ability.

From the Hamilton Spectator, Nov. 11th, 1868.

Book-keeping is not easily learned theoretically, but the volume goes as far as any we have seen to supply the wants of practical experience. The author has taken great pains to explain his system, and he has added a Compendium of valuable Mercantile information which cannot but prove useful.

From the Ottawa Citizen, 16th Nov., 1868.

The author, Mr. Wm. R. Orr, is a practical Accountant, and teacher of many years standing. He has succeeded in producing an ADMIRABLE TEXT BOOK The work is more progressive than any we have seen; it begins at the beginning, and proceeds by regular gradations, until it reaches the highest order and most intricate description of accounts.

From the Canadian Journal of Commerce, 20th Nov., 1868.

The distinguished features of the plan of instruction is that it is progressive. We cannot speak too highly of the pains-taking care and THOROUGH MASTERY of the subject manifested in the production of this work.

From the Cobourg World, 20th Nov., 1868.

We think the Dominion Accountant superior to any other work of the kind extant. It is calculated to take the lead among works in Book-keeping, and we recommend those interested in the study to take a look through it.

From the Newmarket Era, 21st Nov., 1868.

In the Dominion Accountant, we consider the author has succeeded in producing a Text Book worthy of an introduction into all public and private Schools. School Teachers should procure the work at the earliest possible moment. IT IS THE MOST PROGRESSIVE AND COMPREHENSIVE WORK ON THE SUBJECT WE HAVE EVER SEEN.

www.ingramcontent.com/pod-product-compliance
Lightning Source LLC
Chambersburg PA
CBHW020804230426
43666CB00007B/844